D0514405

Further Modern Rope Techniques

Also by Nigel Shepherd:

A MANUAL OF MODERN ROPE TECHNIQUES

Frontispiece: Well prepared for an MIA assessment!

Nigel Shepherd

Further modern rope techniques

with special information for SPA & MIA

Constable · London

First published in Great Britain 1998
by Constable and Company Limited
3 The Lanchesters
162 Fulham Palace Road
London W6 9ER
Copyright © 1998 Nigel Shepherd
The right of Nigel Shepherd to be identified
as the author of this work has been asserted by him
in accordance with the
Copyright, Designs and Patents Act 1988
ISBN 0 09 478540 6
Set in Palastino 9 pt by
CentraCet, Cambridge
Printed in Great Britain by
St Edmundsbury Press Ltd
Bury St Edmunds, Suffolk

A CIP catalogue record for this book
is available from the British Library

Rock climbing, ice climbing and other aspects of mountaineering are inherently dangerous and the techniques described in this book require considerable practice before they can be implemented safely and efficiently on crag and mountain. The techniques require careful judgement, which can only be based on long experience.

We strongly advise that anyone wishing to practice the techniques described herein should do so under the expert tuition of a qualified professional and must recognise the risks that are involved and personally accept the responsibility associated with those risks.

Contents

List of Illustrations

Notes on Photography

The pictures have been staged to show the set-up for each rope technique in the clearest form possible. To achieve this, clutter has been eliminated by omitting harnesses in many of the pictures. I have replaced the harness in such pictures with a quick draw to depict the tie on point. This is not to be interpreted as a tie on to the abseil loop of the harness unless a karabiner is shown. Where the rope is tied through the quick draw you must assume that this is representative of the harness tie on loops through which you would normally thread the rope when tying on.

Acknowledgements

Whilst the words in this book are entirely my own, I cannot claim full credit for the information offered.

The topics discussed are so diverse in character and there are so many differing ways to do things that it is sometimes difficult to stand back from the task in hand to obtain a realistic and unbiased overview of the work. To this end I am indebted to many, but particularly to Nick Banks and Steve Long who kindly gave of their time to read through the manuscript; to Graham MacMahon who was always incredibly enthusiastic about bouncing ideas around and came up with a host of useful suggestions and who helped with some of the pictures – he probably wished he didn't live so close by; to Martin Atkinson of Wild Country who very kindly donated all of the gear used in the photographs; to Mark, Wyn and David at Cambrian Photography in Colwyn Bay who patiently answered an endless barrage of questions and offered kindly advice.

Introduction

It is now eleven years since the publication of *Self Rescue Techniques for Climbers and Instructors* and eight years since Constable first published *A Manual of Modern Rope Techniques*. Over the intervening period there has been little in the way of radical innovation in rope techniques, though some development and refinement has, just as it is hoped it always will, taken place.

There has, however, been a considerable increase in the numbers of participants in outdoor activities and particularly rock climbing. Some sources estimate that there are as many as half a million people who own climbing equipment. Of these climbers there are a great many who spend their time introducing others to the sport through clubs, courses, climbing walls and a whole gamut of other means.

To ensure good practice by these instructors and to offer an element of training and certification, the UKMTB (United Kingdom Mountain Training Board) generates a number of schemes which include the Single Pitch Award (SPA) and the Mountain Instructor Award (MIA). The number of registrations and the popularity of these schemes exceeded all expectations and the total number of registrations since their inception now stands at more than 15,000. In *Further Modern Rope Techniques* I hope to offer a source of reference for all those who have undertaken the various awards and for those who might register in the future.

And there is a great deal more besides. There are some techniques that weren't covered in great detail in *A Manual of Modern Rope Techniques* and new ones that have evolved, improvements to others, some new gadgets and a host of other thoughts and ideas. This book should provide a handy reference, along with the earlier manual (referred to here for brevity as vol. one) on just about all the rope techniques you are likely to need in day to day climbing, instruction and improvised rescue.

Within these pages you will find a variety of techniques described. The book is not intended to be the definitive tome on the subject, for there are numerous ways to do things. You will also doubtless discover that the application of each technique in any given situation will present idiosyncracies not covered in the text. These are so numerous that it would be impossible to list all in a book of this type. Neither do I consider it desirable to do so, for there are things that are best learnt the hard way. I do hope though, that what is offered here is simple and straightforward practical advice on which to base one's efforts and that it will prove useful to many people but, more importantly, help anyone who reads it to climb and instruct safely.

During the intervening years since the publication of the first book I have received many comments on a whole range of techniques. These have proved immensely helpful and I hope that they will continue to land on my doorstep from time to time.

Enjoy your climbing!

Nigel Shepherd
North Wales, 1998

1 The SPA, MIA and MIC

There have been instructor awards in this country for more than five decades. In the very beginning the Mountaineering Association employed instructors and gave them an in-house qualification. This led eventually to the introduction of the Mountaineering Instructor Certificate (MIC) (now the Mountain Instructor Certificate) and the Advanced certificate (MIAC). During the formative years of the qualifications there were very few active professional instructors who earned their living entirely by their trade – quite the reverse of today!

The Mountain Leaders Certificate (now the Mountain Leader Award) followed on, bridging the gap between those who wanted only to take walking groups into the hills and those wishing to become involved in rock climbing.

During the 1970s Outdoor Pursuits Centres proliferated throughout the country and alongside this growth it was inevitable that there would be a vast increase in the number of full time instructors. Gradually the demand for qualification increased.

The origins of the Single Pitch Award (SPA), originally called the Single Pitch Supervisors Award (SPSA) but changed when the Scottish Mountain Leader Training Board joined the scheme, go back to the early 1980s. At this time there were a number of people working in outdoor activities who identified a need for some sort of measure of competence for those taking groups onto crags and who introduce others to the sport of rock climbing. A number of local authority schemes were already in operation but it was felt that something nationally recognised was required. The BMC Training Committee deliberated long and hard about the direction they should take and at the conclusion of discussions it was decided to publish simple guidelines on what should be considered good and safe practice on single pitch rock climbing venues.

For many this was an unsatisfactory state of affairs and, though it fulfilled part of an obligation, it didn't quite go far enough. In 1992 the newly formed UKMTB established a training and certification programme specifically targeted at those taking groups on to single pitch rock climbing venues. From the outset it was envisaged that this would be a very basic qualification, attainable by anyone who has a genuine interest in and a commitment to the sport of rock climbing and who gives time over to introduce others to the sport – for financial reward or otherwise

Around the same time the MIC underwent considerable changes. The most far reaching of these was to split the qualification into two separate components. The Mountain Instructor Award is aimed at those who wish to instruct mountaineering skills in summer only and the Mountain Instructor Certificate is an add-on for those who also wish to instruct winter climbing skills. Prior to these changes being introduced the award of the MIC was only attainable by those with considerable experience in both summer and winter disciplines. The flood gates opened and within a few years more than 500 people registered for the MIA scheme, thus proving a need and at the same time satisfying the demand.

This brief historical perspective is important to understanding the differences between the various qualifications and putting the skills of ropework into some kind of comprehensible perspective. Whilst some techniques will undoubtedly cross over from one qualification to the other, it should be made clear that the levels of competence required to attain each award are significantly different, as is the experience of the participant.

The syllabus of the SPA is intended to offer training and qualification for those who wish to instruct on single pitch climbing venues only. The definition of single pitch is any crag that is:

- climbed without intermediate stances
- described as a single pitch in the guidebook
- allows students to be lowered to the ground at all times
- is non-tidal
- is non-serious and has little objective danger
- presents no difficulties on approach or retreat, such as route finding, scrambling or navigation.

As part of their assessment candidates are required to demonstrate their ability to lead on Severe grade rock and to be able to place sound running belays and to arrange a good stance at the top of the climb. This requirement ensures that all those undertaking the scheme are committed rock climbers and have a good understanding of the sport.

Candidates are also assessed on their ability to solve problems. These are in general very straightforward and will not involve complex rope manoeuvres or major cliff evacuations.

A part of the scheme is dedicated to climbing wall use and the supervision of groups. Many climbing walls now require anyone bringing a group for instruction to have the SPA as a minimum level of competence. This is a reliable yardstick and reassures the management that those under supervision are being well looked after.

The MIA is an altogether more comprehensive award. In addition to the skills required for the SPA, candidates for this scheme are required to demonstrate their ability to take care of and instruct on multi-pitch climbs up to Very Severe standard. The teaching element also includes the ability to instruct students in the skills of leading and the complexities of safe ropework. They will also be asked to solve much more complex rescue scenarios that may require multi pitch evacuation of the cliff with an injured climber.

The award also requires that they be competent to lead people on scrambling terrain, either as a day out in its own right, part of a mountain day or when the techniques of short roping are required in descent from a rock climb.

The MIC is an add-on component to the MIA and successful completion of this allows instructors to instruct and lead in winter conditions, including climbs up to Grade III standard.

Beyond these qualifications is that of Mountain Guide. To achieve this award candidates must be experienced and competent mountaineers in every respect. They will be required to demonstrate their ability to teach and guide to a high standard, both in the UK in all seasons and in the Alps, both on foot and on ski.

There are very clear differences between all the awards in terms of what is required of candidates. A common thread binds them – that whatever rope technique is required must be used competently and safely, there is no allowable margin of error when you are responsible for people's well-being and enjoyment.

2 Top Roping and Bottom Roping

On single pitch climbing venues you will either choose to safeguard those in your care from the top of the crag or to have the rope doubled through an anchor at the top of the crag and belay climbers from the bottom.

Each method has its merits and for that matter, its draw-backs. If you have a group to take out for the day, belaying from the bottom of the crag will enable you, as the instructor, to keep more people actively involved for more of the time. It is possible to arrange two or three climbs to take place simultaneously and you flit backwards and forwards between each group making sure that each is conducted safely. If you belay from the top of the crag it is very unlikely that you will be able to entertain more than one novice climber at a time.

Using a bottom rope belaying system means that you can allow the group to belay each other. Whilst one of them is climbing, two or three others can be responsible for belaying. Thus two climbs might conceivably actively involve up to eight people at any one time. There is much to be said in favour of this, not least that everyone will feel a part of the activity by working together, and they are much less likely to lose interest.

The major drawback with the technique of bottom roping is that it has a profound effect on the environment by concentrat-ing a large number of people in one place, causing considerable erosion to both the rock and to the ground immediately below a climb. It is also rather invasive, limiting access to the routes that you are using for others who may wish to climb them. You should always be considerate in your use of the crags and allow others to climb the routes that you are on by vacating them as quickly as possible.

In such a situation you, as the instructor, will have an

enormous responsibility to ensure that everything is done safely and that no-one gets hurt by tomfoolery or neglect or carelessness. To organise two climbs at the same time you must choose routes that are close enough together that it takes only a second or two for you to move from one to the other. In that way you are more likely to be able to keep control of the situation. To have three climbs on the go at the same time is much more difficult to manage and with complete beginners may not be practicable nor, indeed, advisable.

RIGGING ANCHORS

In order to set up a bottom roping system you will first need to go to the top of the crag and arrange the anchor points. It is very important to ensure that the anchors are solid. Unless it is a big stout tree, firmly established, or a large purpose-designed anchor, it is preferable to select more than one anchor.

One anchor point is only suitable if the climb is immediately below it and any load from below will be directed straight on to the anchor. If there is the slightest chance that a falling climber will swing off to one side, two anchor points (minimum) will be needed in order to stabilise the direction of pull. Such simplistic situations are unfortunately rare and it is more common to find that anchor points are well off to the side of where you would like them to be.

You will need to have the fixing point of the climbing rope draped over the edge of the crag. The ideal that you should strive for is to arrange things so that the climber does not have to go over the top of the crag but can climb up until they can just touch the karabiner that secures their safety rope. From that moment the belayers can take the weight of the climber and lower him or her back down to the bottom of the crag.

It is therefore necessary to have anchors that are well back from the edge and to use a rope to connect them all to one central point which is then draped over the top of the crag. If the only suitable anchors are to be found close to the edge it is better to set up the bottom roping system so that the end of the climb is well out of arm's reach of the anchor points.

When you construct an anchor point in this way, the position at which the climbing rope is attached may be subjected to considerable movement across the rock. If you do not take account of this the rope could very quickly become chaffed and worn through to the extent that it is damaged beyond further use. Similarly, the rope that is used for climbing on may be subjected to the same chaffing effect. There is a need to keep a regular check to see that all remains safe throughout the activity.

To get around this problem you can place something between the rock and the ropes so that it is protected. The most effective padding to use is a piece of hard-wearing carpet which, if you tie cord through the ends, can be secured in place by attaching it to the anchor.

Regardless of how many anchor points you select they should all be connected together to come to one central point. This is most easily achieved by using a length of rope to construct the whole anchor. It is advisable to use a non-stretch rope for this. A climbing rope has lots of stretch in it – this is necessary to help it absorb shock in a fall. If used to connect a number of anchors together it will create an anchor point that has a certain amount of stretch in it. This stretch will be accentuated when a climber's weight comes on to the climbing rope and the attachment point at the edge of the crag will rub up and down the rock. This chaffing of the rope will cause considerable wear and tear and may, in an extreme case, cut through the rope.

By using a non-stretch rope this problem is largely eliminated. Furthermore, this type of rope is much more hard-wearing. It is worth making the point here that non-stretch ropes should not be used as climbing rope, as they do not have the same elasticity as climbing ropes. The shock loading on the anchors and belay system is considerably greater in the event of a fall and might result in bodily injury or anchor failure.

The only exception to this is perhaps on the sandstone outcrops of southern England where climbs are very short and considerable erosion is caused by ropes seesawing back and forth over the edge of the outcrop. Also, the rock is so abrasive that ordinary climbing ropes wear out very quickly indeed.

There are a number of ways to bring multiple anchors to one central point. Photo 1 illustrates a suitable method. The all important factor to remember whichever method you use is that if one should fail there must be no shock loading on the remaining anchors.

Obviously, the more anchors you have, the more rope you will need to connect them. It may be possible to connect two anchors together with a sling to create one attachment point in which case you will save on rope. Photos 2 and 3 show different methods of using a sling to bring two anchors to one point. (See vol. one for other suggestions.)

Getting the tension to each anchor can be a bit problematical. One way to make it easier is to tie the end of the rope into the first anchor. Having done that, clip a large karabiner into the abseil loop on your harness and clip the rope into it. Take the rope to the next anchor and clip it in. Now clip back through the krab on your abseil loop and take the rope to the next anchor. Keep going like this until you have clipped all the anchors. Using tension off the criss cross of ropes that you have, move to the position in which you want the anchor ropes to be. You'll need to feed them all through the krab on your abseil loop as you move. Once you are satisfied that they are all under tension and in position, make some final adjustments, take the whole bunch of ropes out of the krab on your harness and tie them all in a great big overhand knot. Photo 4 shows a simplified version.

To be certain that the tension remains equal throughout, you

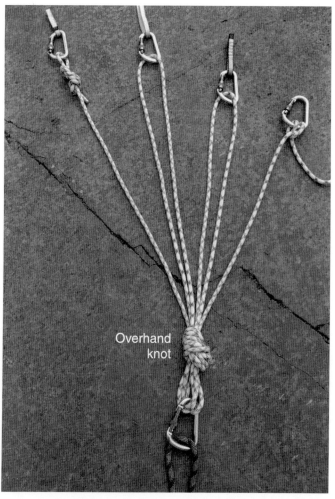

Overhand
knot

1 Using the rope to bring multiple anchors to one central point.

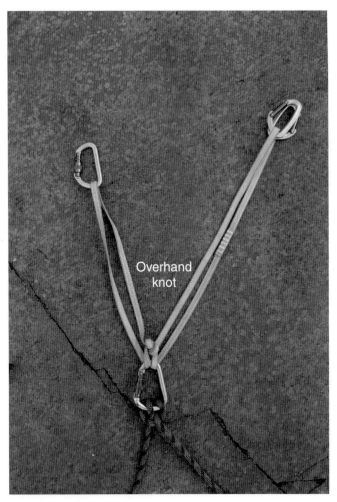

Overhand
knot

2 Two anchors brought to one point using a sling with an overhand knot in the middle.

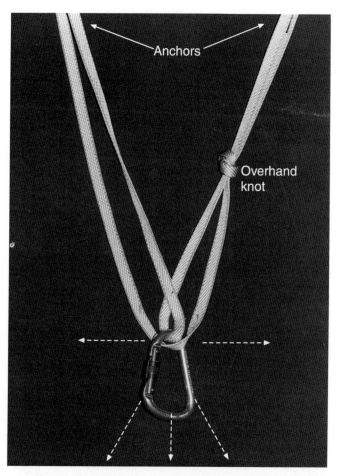

3 Two anchors brought to one point, allowing for sideways movement but retaining equal load on both. Tie an overhand in both sides to reduce shock loading if one should fail.

can return to each anchor point and secure the rope with a clove hitch – though it is not at all important to do this.

The loops formed by the large overhand knot may be too bulky to accommodate a karabiner safely. If this is the case, divide the ropes equally between a couple of screwgate krabs.

This will be your attachment point for the climbing rope. The karabiner or karabiners that you use here will be subjected to considerable wear and tear against the rock. Ideally, use steel screwgates or, as previously suggested, use a piece of carpet to stop them rubbing directly on the rock.

Clip the karabiners in so that the gates face uppermost and the opening end points down the crag. Sometimes karabiner screwgates can rattle themselves undone, but if you place them this way they are much less likely to do so. Another method of attaching the climbing rope to the anchor uses a large figure eight descendeur (photo 5). This method has clear safety advantages in that there is no possibility of a karabiner undoing itself or one of your students unclipping accidentally. Unfortunately, the rope runs against the rock during taking in and lowering creating a more serious abrasive action, as well as more friction. Using this method it is important to place carpet protection between the rope and rock. It is a particularly suitable method to use if the anchor point hangs freely over the edge of the crag.

If you don't have a spare rope available for rigging anchors together to one central point you will have to use slings. Be very careful to ensure that the tension is equally divided amongst the anchor points. It would appear to be a straight-forward task but it is usually not so easy to achieve as satisfactory a result as is possible with a separate rope. If you have to connect slings together because they are not long enough, you will need to use screwgate krabs at each connection. Some people lark's-foot slings together to create extra length but this is not as safe or reliable as using karabiners.

If you need to shorten slings it is possible to do so by tying

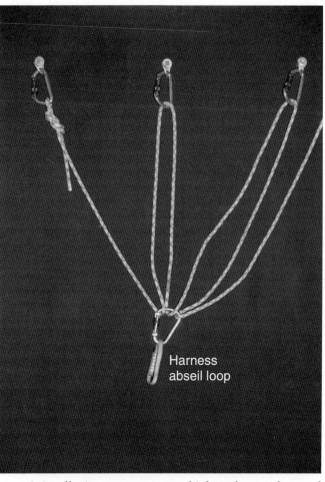

Harness
abseil loop

4 An effective system to get multiple anchors under equal
tension.

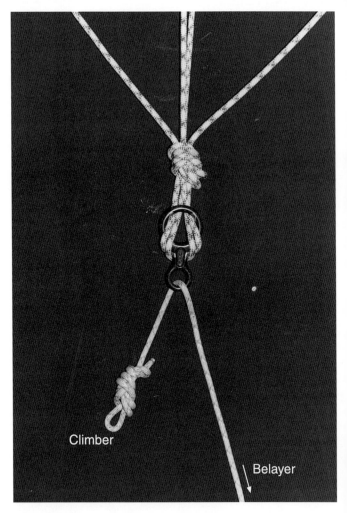

Climber

Belayer

5 Figure eight descendeur used in place of screwgate karabiner at anchor point. Note that ropes will rub against the rock unless anchor point is hanging free.

an overhand or figure eight knot to achieve the desired length.

Occasionally, the anchors may not be situated in the most desirable line for the anticipated loading. In such cases it is possible to place a directional anchor, preferably anchors, to hold the attachment point in position. Whilst these anchors will not bear the brunt of the force or load, they should nonetheless be as solid as the main anchors. A sideways pull can generate a fair amount of force and, of course, if the anchors come out unexpectedly under the load, the climber may swing and sustain an injury. Photo 6 shows a suggestion for retaining directional stability.

Personal safety whilst rigging anchors or working close to the edge of a crag is paramount. You should always ensure that you are tied into an anchor of some description even if it has to be on a long cow's tail to permit free movement across the top of the crag. At assessment, personal safety is an important aspect of overall performance.

TOP ROPING

To set up an anchor for belaying from the top of the crag you must observe one or two important principles of safety.

Firstly, you should arrange your position so that you can see the climb in its entirety and secondly you must be directly above the climber you are belaying. This ideal is not always achievable and some situations may necessitate dropping down to a ledge below the edge of the crag. If you are not able to position yourself so that anyone you bring up the climb can move off easily to safe ground before untying from the rope, you might have to consider lowering them back down to the ground.

It is well worth considering belaying climbers with a direct belay. This method has a number of advantages over the more traditional method of belaying off your harness. It means that you are not committed to take the full weight of the climber if

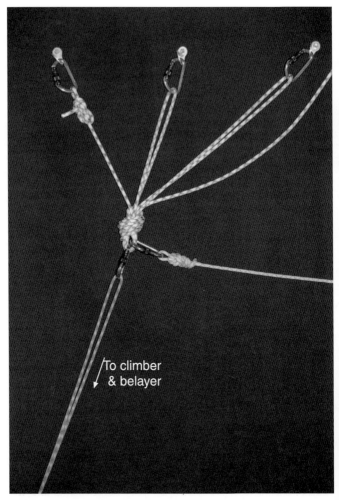

To climber
& belayer

6 Side tension anchor for stabilising main anchor.

he or she falls off. Neither will you have to 'escape from the system' if a problem occurs. It goes without saying that your anchor points should be one hundred per cent solid for a direct belay, as the load will be transmitted directly to the anchors. A similar anchor set-up at the top of the crag to that used for arranging a bottom rope is therefore quite sensible. For comfort, safety and ease of operation the attachment point for the belaying method ought to be slightly above you and well back from the edge of the crag. This precludes the use of a belay plate because you need to operate such a device from behind. Normally you would use an Italian hitch or a descendeur, both of which can be safely operated from below.

When using a direct belaying method in this way you must take care of your own personal safety by clipping yourself in to the anchor point as well. This should be done separately by means of a sling or 'cow's tail'. Snake slings, which have a number of sections separated by bar-tack stitching, are particularly useful for this, as you can adjust your position very easily when needed. Photo 7 shows a suggested set-up clearly.

If you choose to belay climbers from within the system you do so in a normal climbing way, but bear in mind the fact that your ability to move around is severely restricted.

BELAYING METHODS FROM BELOW

As stated earlier, bottom roping systems are infinitely preferable because they involve more people. With only a short demonstration and explanation of important safety considerations you can let the group belay each other – provided that you are on hand to oversee the whole operation.

Arranging the rope through an anchor point at the top of the climb will generate a certain amount of friction that helps the belayers hold the rope. In this situation any loading of the rope will create an upward-pulling force on the belayers and this should be taken into account. If you have light people belaying heavier climbers you may need to arrange an anchor that will prevent them being pulled up the cliff if the climber falls off. Such anchors may not always be found easily, in which case you might decide to use other participants to add extra weight to the belayer. They can be clipped together with slings from the front of the harness into the back of the harness of the person in front of them.

If suitable upward-pulling anchors are readily available the belayer only need be clipped in. Arrange the attachment so that any load generated by holding a climber is transmitted fairly directly through the belayer and on to the anchor.

Belayers should be positioned close in to the crag to avoid the possibility that a load might drag them in towards the bottom of the cliff. If the nature of the terrain dictates that you have to belay away from the bottom of the crag it is essential to tie the belayer into an upward-pulling anchor.

There are a number of ways to utilise as many people as possible in the belaying. One person should be attached to the belay device and be the main operator. Another can stand at the bottom of the crag facing out and pull down on the rope as the climber moves up. The belayer takes the rope through the belay device and there should always be another person acting as safety back-up on the dead or controlling rope.

The type of belay device or system that you use is entirely one of personal choice. The Gri Gri is a very good device for novices to use as it will lock even if everyone lets go. Some climbers, with long experience, find the device a little awkward to use at first and the temptation is to dismiss it out of hand. If you are teaching people who have never used any other device to use the Gri Gri, you will find that most will pick up the basic principles quite quickly. The Italian hitch is also a good method, as is any modern belay device. Be wary of using older style Sticht plates, as they have a tendency to jam up at the least convenient moment. See Chapter 8 on Belaying (page 132) for ways to operate these devices.

When instructing the use of a belay system, teach a method that is fairly simple to understand. The most important aspect is that the belayers must not let go of the dead rope or controlling rope. You can work out your own methodology for this – many people have their own particular way to do things. Brief everyone on what is to happen during the climb; as soon as the climber reaches the end of the climb; and whilst the climber is being lowered back to the ground. Before any lowering can take place the climber should place all of his or her weight on the rope. The belayers lock off the rope whilst the climber does this. Once you are satisfied that all the weight is on the rope the belayers can begin lowering very slowly. Do not allow any rope to run suddenly through the device. If you do let rope run quickly the climber may experience the feeling that the rope has been let go and will try to grab hold of the rock taking their weight off the rope. The lowering should only be speeded up once the climber has got used to the sensation of being lowered with someone else in control of their destiny.

Whatever system you choose to use it is vitally important that you remain in a position where you can control and supervise everyone involved, continually emphasising the importance of safety.

DEALING WITH PROBLEMS

Few problems are likely to occur that are not solved easily and simply. Probably the most common occurrence of all is that of 'stuck' climber. This happens mainly through fear or lack of experience to see what can and cannot be used as a handhold or foothold. Sometimes it occurs through outright fear and the climber becomes 'frozen' to the rock face. In both cases a solution may be simply to talk the climber through a sequence of moves or to encourage with sympathetic words. If, on the other hand, the climber has managed somehow to get a foot or a knee jammed in a crack you will almost certainly have to go to their assistance. One of the more unusual incidents I have experienced was a solidly jammed helmet!

Anyone who is stuck or refuses to move and will not take their weight on the rope to be lowered back to the ground will require you to go to their assistance. This could be done by going around to the top of the crag and abseiling down by their side to talk them through the sequence or cajole them into being lowered. To do this will take quite a bit of time and take you away from your responsibilities to the rest of the group.

It is better to go to their assistance from below. One way to do this is as follows. Put a French prusik knot on to the live climbing rope just above the belayer and attach it to the abseil loop on your own harness. Move the prusik up the rope until you can lean out on it, putting tension on the rope in a counter balance situation. Having done this you can put a second prusik, such as a Klemheist, below the first and ascend the rope.

An alternative and very quick system is to attach a belay device below the first French prusik. If the rock is low angled you can simply walk up the rock taking in the rope through the belay device as you gain height. Make sure that the belayers give you some slack but don't ask them to take the rope out of the belay device completely. Photo 8 shows this set-up. Note that on easy angled rock the foot loop prusik may not even be necessary.

As you move up the French prusik will release itself but will act as an autobloc to prevent you slipping back down if you have to let go of the rope. Be careful though, French prusik knots do not always lock without a little assistance to start the process. Once you get to the stuck climber you can lean back on the prusik and ask the belayers to take the rope tight through the belay device and lock it off. This is by way of a back up. You are now in a position to talk the stuck climber through the moves and being by the side of them may be sufficient moral encouragement to do this. As they move up

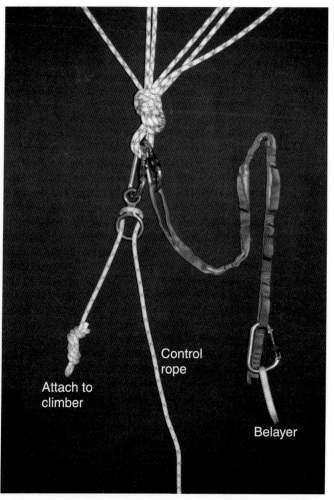

Attach to climber

Control rope

Belayer

7 Top roping set-up.

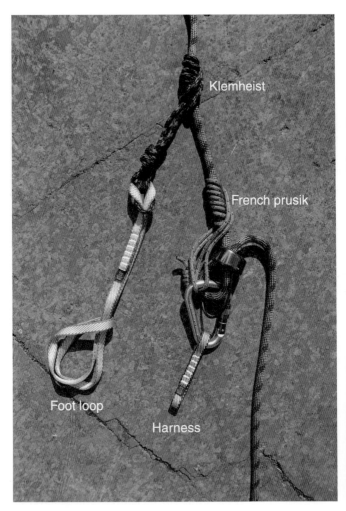

8 Ascending set-up to rescue 'stuck' climber.

9 Bottom roping. The anchor point has been arranged over the edge to reduce erosion.

10 Bottom roping. It is easier to supervise two groups when climbs are close together.

you can continue to ascend alongside, taking in the rope through the belay device as you move up, using your weight against theirs as a counter balance. If this fails and they do not want to climb on or be lowered down alone, you can clip into their harness tie on loop or the abseil loop and go down with them in an accompanied abseil. All you need to do is simply connect yourself to the tie on loop of their harness – a quick draw will do – and abseil down to the ground with them. Don't forget to ask the belayer to take the rope out of their belay device before you begin to descend.

All the time that you are doing this you will still of course be responsible for ensuring the safety of any other ropes that you may have set up, but at least you will never be out of sight of what is going on. Of course, if something major were to go awry on another climb it would take you some time to get there to render assistance. If you are on your own supervising the group it may be preferable to call a temporary halt to the other climb whilst you sort out the problem in hand.

If by some unlucky coincidence a climber is injured whilst on the route, the same method can be used to go to their assistance and descend to the ground under your control.

This is by far the simplest way to deal with a stuck climber. There are some others. For example, if you are using a Gri Gri, there is no need for a prusik. You could take over the belayer's Gri Gri by clipping yourself into the karabiner that attaches it to their harness and unclipping them from it. You can ascend the rope pulling the slack through the Gri Gri as you ascend and you can, with practice, use the Gri Gri as an abseiling device.

Keep it simple! is the key to solving these sorts of problems, for simplicity often means speed and efficiency.

3 Abseiling with Groups

Abseiling is perceived by many to be a fun activity and may in some cases be set up entirely divorced from the sport of rock climbing to which it rightly belongs.

In itself there is nothing wrong with this philosophy but there are wider implications if it is used by non-climbers who do not understand the technical aspects of rock climbing ropework.

There are a number of important considerations to bear in mind when choosing a suitable venue. Of greatest significance is accessibility. The group will be much easier to control if you are able to arrange for them to wait well back from the edge of the crag but when they need to come forward to take their turn they are not exposed to the risk of falling over the cliff edge as they approach and before being attached to a safety rope.

Take time to consider the situation at the bottom of the crag too. Ideally this should be fairly flat and free of danger. If you don't have anyone to supervise the group at the bottom of the crag you will need to position them in a place where you are able to keep an eye on them. It is also important to move them away from the foot of the abseil out of line of fire of anything that might accidentally be knocked down the crag.

You may decide that you want people to return to the top of the crag after they have disconnected from the rope. To this end, try to choose a venue that has an easy and obvious walking route back to the top.

For people, young or older, who have never abseiled before choose a crag that is not too steep. Vertical and overhanging crags are intimidating places for those not familiar with a crag environment and people may become preoccupied with their fear rather than concentrating on and being able to savour the experience. Neither should the crag be too high, about 10–15 metres is ideal. This height means that you will be able to get people down an abseil many times. The more they do, the more confident they will become and you can move on to more exciting things more quickly.

SAFETY

First experiences of abseiling necessitate the use of a safety rope. This is not only a sensible precaution but is also a great confidence booster. The safety rope should either be tied in directly to the harness as per the manufacturer's recommendation or clipped in to the abseil loop of the harness with a screwgate karabiner. Normally, this would be attached to the loop below the abseil device. Photo 11 shows the basic set-up.

It is also advisable to set up the abseil rope so that it can be released under load. More problems arise in group abseiling situations than they do in 'normal' abseiling by experienced climbers when it is used as a means of descent.

The main problems that occur include clothing stuck in the abseil device or, much worse, hair, which can be extremely painful. Paying close attention to these potential disasters prior to launching off will pay dividends and avoid the possibility that they might occur in the first instance. Another common occurrence is that the abseiler becomes so terrified that they are unable to complete the descent and, just as in climbing up, the abseiler may become 'frozen' to the rock face. Occasionally, someone might get their foot or leg jammed in a crack. In rare cases, the abseil device may become jammed or a knot appear in the rope.

If such problems do occur you will be well placed to deal with them if you set up a releasable abseil.

It is very simple to set up. Instead of securing the abseil rope with a figure eight knot directly to the anchor, connect it with an Italian hitch into an HMS karabiner clipped into the anchor. Tie off the Italian hitch securely with an appropriate method (see vol. one, page 21). If someone has a problem on the abseil

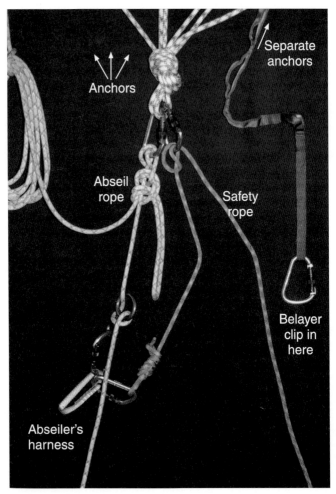

11 Basic set-up of releasable abseil.

you are then able to release the rope and take the strain on to the safety rope. This can be effected very quickly, a particularly important factor if someone gets their hair caught in a device when there is considerable urgency to act. Photo 12 shows the detail of the tied off Italian hitch in a realeasable abseil.

You should operate the safety rope as a direct belay and keep yourself out of the system. Obviously you must be tied in to the anchor but it is a good idea to allow yourself some room for manoeuvre and tie in with a long cow's tail. A snake sling is particularly useful for this (photo 11).

An Italian hitch is a good enough method with which to operate the safety rope. So also is a figure eight descendeur. Both of these belay methods allow you to stand in front of the anchor where you can be most useful. Belay devices have to be operated from behind and are therefore not so convenient.

SIMPLE RESCUE SCENARIOS

By proper planning and setting up most problems are easily avoided. If something unforeseen does occur, it is preferable to solve it by working to the principle of 'simplest is quickest'. Do not get bogged down in overly complex solutions to problems.

For example, if an abseiler gets clothing stuck in an abseil device lock off the safety rope (as in photo 12 or in photo 57 vol. one) and then release the abseil rope until there is enough slack for them to pull the clothing out of the device. The safety rope can just be held tightly by hand without the need to tie it off, but you will have to work quickly. If you want to ensure there is a safety back up you could put a French prusik on the loaded safety rope and attach it to the anchor or tie off the device you are using to safeguard them with. (Provided you don't have to move too far away from the anchor, you could always have a French prusik safety back up on the safety rope for those just-in-case situations.)

Once the victim has released the clothing from the device

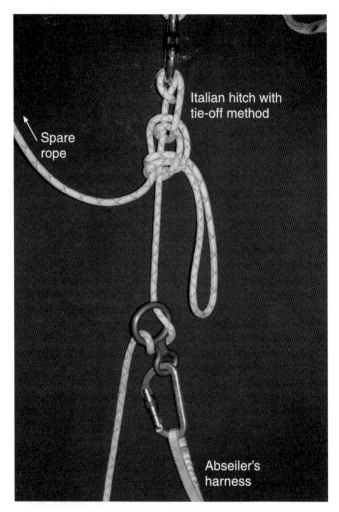

Italian hitch with
tie-off method

Spare
rope

Abseiler's
harness

12 Detail of Italian hitch tie off in releasable abseil.

you can take in the abseil rope tight, tie it off again, and continue with the abseil by lowering the victim's weight back on to the abseil rope, using the safety rope.

Hair caught in a device requires extremely quick action on your part and there may not be enough time to tie off the safety rope until you have released the abseil. Just so long as you have a tight hold on the safety and work with speed this has to be acceptable.

If someone is stuck, terrified and refusing to move any further, you should, to begin with, make every effort to talk them down. Words of comfort and encouragement are often the best solution to this type of problem. If words should meet with little success you might try taking over control of their descent yourself. This can be done by lowering both the safety and the abseil ropes simultaneously. You must ensure that the abseiler's full weight remains on one or both ropes at all times. If you allow slack to develop, the shock of falling back on to the rope before it becomes loaded may be too discouraging and frightening. It will be obvious here that you should ensure there is sufficient abseil rope available to achieve this, though of course you could always allow the abseil rope to fall to the ground, as there will always be sufficient length of safety rope.

If someone is so terrified that even this solution proves unworkable, or they have a foot stuck in a crack, the best option is to go down and help them abseil. A suggested way to do this safely is as follows.

Take all the load on to the safety rope and secure it by tying it off. Release enough of the abseil rope so that you can attach yourself and then tie it off again. Connect yourself to the abseil rope using a long sling shortened to make one long attachment and one short. Make sure that you include a safety back up French prusik attached to your leg loop. Then release yourself from the cow's tail attachment to the anchor. Abseil down to the victim and disconnect them from their abseil device. Remove it from the rope.

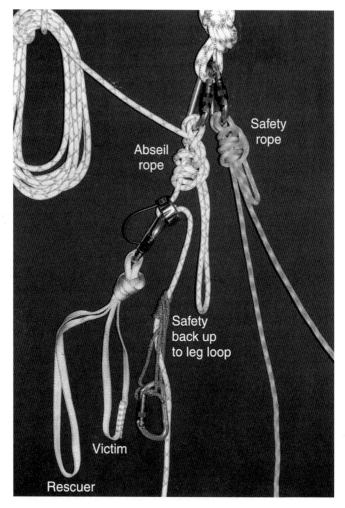

13 Rescue set-up for 'stuck' abseiler.

Next, connect the abseil loop of their harness on to the short loop from your own abseil rig. When you do this, try to lift the victim up a little, so that the safety rope connection goes slack. If you think they are able, you could ask them to pull themselves up on one of the ropes. Once you have the victim secured to your abseil device you can unclip them from the safety rope. Abseil down together to the ground (Photo 13).

An alternative to the method suggested would be to use an entirely separate rope for your own abseil. You may decide to set one up ready 'just in case'. The method of rescue is identical to that previously described.

By far the most important factor is that you must not become involved in unnecessary and overly complex solutions.

4 MIA

Improvised Rescue

Many of the techniques required for the MIA, particularly improvised rescue, are covered in vol. one. There are, however, one or two other aspects not dealt with there and others where there have been additional techniques or improvements made to existing ones.

IMPROVISED RESCUE

A great deal of emphasis is placed on the ability to conduct rescues from crags using only normal climbing equipment. Placing such importance on these skills not only allows the instructor to operate with confidence in the knowledge that they possess but it also presents an opportunity to hone rope techniques and develop a greater understanding of the principles of good stance organisation, selection of anchors and avoidance of basic problems.

It is important to recognise from the outset that the simplest solution to a problem is very often the most efficient and that to embark on complex and long-winded fanciful rope manoeuvres may not be the most appropriate way to solve a problem.

For example, a client or student who is having difficulty on a section of a climb may need some help getting over the hard bit. To effect this the instructor might rig a simple assisted hoist. If the instructor, however, feels strong enough to do it, they may just simply pull the client hand over hand. Obviously, the rope needs to be taken in through the belay device so that security at all times is assured, but there is absolutely nothing wrong with this solution.

Another example might be in the case of forced evacuation

from the crag. If you are able to get down to the ground in one abseil or lower, even if it means tying two ropes together, it is preferable to fix the rope in place, retreat and recover your equipment at a later stage. Obviously, if you are likely to need your gear further down the mountain or you are in a remote spot, you will need to retrieve as much of it as possible on the way down.

SOLVING SIMPLE PROBLEMS

At assessment you will normally be asked to solve a number of simple and common problems in addition, to at least one major scenario. Simple problems include the following:

A knot in the rope

If, despite all your careful preparations, you discover an overhand knot in the climbing rope between you and your client, either while leading a pitch or while taking in the rope, it will be necessary to either undo it or, more straightforward, move it down the rope. If your client has a rope attached to a second client the best thing to do is to ask them to move the knot down the rope until it reaches their tie on knot. Once the client reaches your stance you can then untie the knot by first clipping them into the belay anchor with a sling and releasing them from the end of the rope. Untie the offending knot and then tie back on to the end of the rope.

A client who is tied on to the end of the rope with no second rope attached can undo the mysterious knot by simply moving it down towards their tie on and then making a large loop to step through in order to undo the offending knot.

In no circumstances should you ask them to untie from the end of the rope whilst you are out of reach and without the ability to check one hundred per cent that they have retied on to the rope end correctly.

Stuck runner

If a client is unable to retrieve a runner from its placement it may be better for you to descend and take the runner out yourself. First of all you should try talking the client through a procedure which you work out from your recall of how the runner was placed. If this fails, the client may well reach a point where the problem is made worse and the runner is beyond retrieval. You may, of course, decide that you are content to leave it behind and carry on with the climb.

If you decide that you will get the runner back yourself, solving the problem is largely one of good organisation. Bring your client or clients up to the stance and secure them to the belay. You may find it quicker to climb back down to the runner to retrieve it. You can ask one of your clients to belay you as you do so and to safeguard you as you climb back up.

You might prefer to arrange your ropes in such a way as you can abseil down to the stuck gear. What you might choose to do is to abseil on the rope between your first and second client and ask the first to belay you on your own rope whilst you descend. Always abseil down with a French prusik back up, as this will allow you to release both hands to retrieve the runner. You can then climb back up the route and your client can take in the rope as you do so.

Another solution is to abseil down and to prusik back up to the stance. You would normally do this on your own rope, without necessarily untying from the end. Simply drop a loop of rope down the crag, enough to reach a little over halfway to the runner and then fix the rope to the anchor. Attach your abseil device to the fixed rope and descend on this. As you go down, the rope attached to your harness will give you the extra distance required to reach the stuck runner.

It is important to work methodically in arranging ropes to descend otherwise you might become horrendously entangled and spend unnecessary time sorting out the mess you have created.

Client climbs past a runner

This is a favourite problem offered by assessors, but in truth it should rarely occur! Arranging your stance so that you have a view of the whole pitch and good communication will prevent this happening. Unfortunately, despite your best efforts, it is inevitable that it will happen occasionally. Clients frequently become so absorbed and focused on the task in hand that they pay little attention to anything other than making the moves. Any time that a client asks for slack rope you should question why they need it. Normally it will be to climb down a little bit but if they say that they need it to climb past a runner then clearly something is amiss. If you are aware of the problem you can prevent them climbing more than a foot or so above the runner and can easily ask them to climb back down until level with the runner. If, however, they climb a good few feet above the problem is altogether more serious and will require prompt action on your part.

If a client were to fall off a few feet above a runner the fall could be quite long and in doing so they might sustain an injury. As soon as you realise there is something amiss you need to ask them to stay exactly where they are whilst you arrange for a loop of rope to be sent down to them. The best thing to do is to tie off the belay device and, using the slack rope from where you are tied in to the anchor, drop a loop down to them. This loop should have a knot and a karabiner in it which the client will clip into the abseil loop of their harness. You attach the rope to the anchor via an Italian hitch and ask them to take their weight on the rope. Lower them back down until level with the runner and regain control of the climbing rope through the belay device. Once they are secured again you can ask them to untie the loop, remove the runner and climb on.

If the client can get into a reasonably comfortable position and can reach the rope that goes between you, the instructor, and the runner below the client, it may be possible for them to pull through a bit of slack rope, tie a figure eight or overhand knot in the rope and clip it in to a screwgate on the harness. Obviously the client must be very comfortable and able to use both hands to tie the knot.

Cannot climb a difficult section of the route

If you are part way up a climb and one of your clients finds it too difficult to do the moves you can assist them by keeping the rope very tight. More often than not you'll be able to help them over the hard bit with assistance from the rope. If this fails, you may have to arrange an assisted hoist. This can be effected without the need to escape from the system. Tie off the belay device and put a French prusik autobloc on the live rope. Drop a loop of the dead rope down to the client with a krab clipped in. This krab is then attached to the client's abseil loop on their harness or just into the tie in loop. Undo the tied off belay device and tension all the ropes. If the client pulls on the only rope that travels downwards and you pull on the spare rope at the same time you will both be able to effect the hoist. See photo 69 in vol. one.

Once the difficult section has been overcome, the client can release the loop of rope and you can regain control through the belay device. If you leave the French prusik on whilst you are sorting out the ropes the client will be safeguarded throughout.

This method of hoisting can only really work if you have enough rope available to implement it. If your client is more than a third of the rope's length below the stance you will need to consider the addition of a sling or slings, connected on to the end of the loop that is dropped to them. If you have enough slings, you could add a considerable length to the loop. Each sling should ideally be connected to another via a screwgate karabiner, though if none is available, lark's-footing slings together may be the best alternative.

Should the client be a long way below or off to one side, where it is impossible to throw them a loop, you may need to effect a hoist from within the system. This is set up in exactly the same way as the hoist shown in vol. one photo 71 where the anchor is replaced by your belay device. This method is obviously laborious and time-consuming and as soon as the client is within reach you should revert to an assisted hoist.

Client fails to follow a pitch

If, despite your best efforts, a client cannot follow a pitch and there is harder climbing further up the route, you might decide it is better to retreat. To do this you will need to lower the client back down to the previous stance and secure them there whilst you arrange to retreat.

If the anchor point on the previous stance was a complex one you may not be able to trust the client to re-rig it. In this case you will probably choose to arrange a counter balance abseil.

Lower the client back to the stance and ask them to stand or sit securely on the ledge. Escape from the system and make sure that the rope to the client is backed up with a tied off Italian hitch to the anchor and leave the French prusik in place. Decide what anchor you are going to use to retreat from. If you have nothing else available this may have to be the anchors that you are tied into. It is preferable, of course, to leave behind the minimum amount of gear so alternatives should be arranged if possible.

It is likely that you will need to leave, at the very least, a sling and krab behind so that the abseil rope can be retrieved easily. Once you have arranged the abseil anchor thread the rope through it and keep pulling it through until it is tight to your client down below. For the moment leave the tied off Italian hitch and French prusik in place. Attach yourself to the rope on the opposite side to the client's rope and make sure that you put on a French prusik back up to the leg loop.

Retrieve all the gear you are not leaving behind, position yourself as closely as possible to the anchor and then untie the Italian hitch back up, clearing any other gear remaining. Pull through any slack rope until you are tight on the rope and heave backwards with all your might! As you heave back you must hold your abseil rope tightly in one hand whilst you release the original French prusik securing the client. Once that is released and recovered you can abseil down to join your client, arrange a suitable anchor for both of you and then retrieve the ropes to continue abseiling down.

If you do not have enough rope to reach the client in one abseil, which will be the case if the pitch was longer than half of the rope length, you will need to abseil down as far as is necessary to create sufficient rope to reach their stance and arrange another abseil anchor to continue your descent to the client.

Photos 14, 15 and 16 show a suggested set-up for the counter balance abseil descent as described. Always remember to tie a knot in the loose end of the rope that you are abseiling on.

Of course, if you are able to lower your client to the ground in one rope length, or even by joining two ropes together, you should do so, for it will be easier to retreat yourself, even if you have to make the descent yourself in two stages. Photo 61 on page 137 of vol. one shows a way to pass a knot through a lowering device using a French prusik. Turn the page upside down for improved clarity!

Other simple problems may be presented to you, but the ability to cope with these described should equip you with the basic knowledge to solve most of them simply and efficiently.

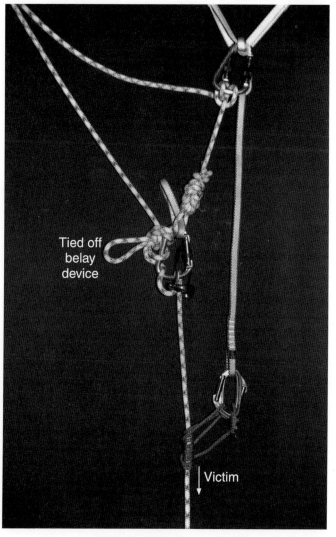

Tied off
belay
device

Victim

14 Escape directly to counter balance: Stage 1.

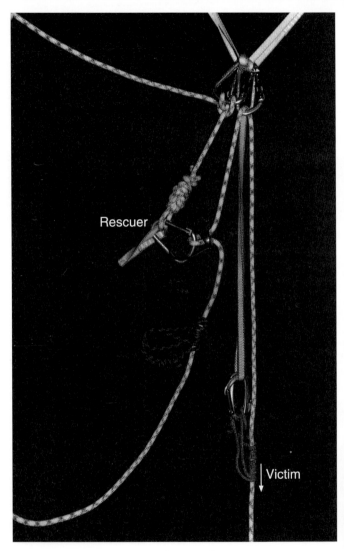

15 Escape directly to counter balance: Stage 2.

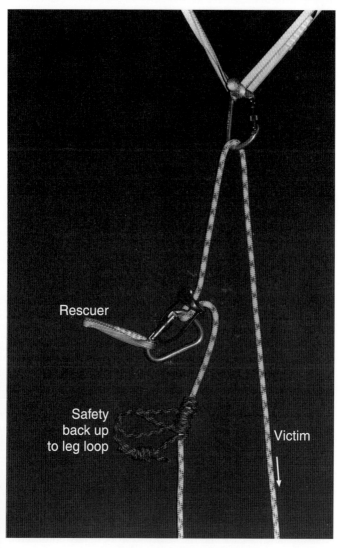

16 Escape directly to counter balance: Stage 3.

COMPLEX SCENARIOS

At assessment you will be given at least one complex rescue problem to solve. The nature of the problem will depend on the type of ground you are climbing on and will generally be something fairly realistic. Assessors have differing ways of presenting and creating these scenarios and it is important for you, as the candidate, to be sure that you understand fully what has been presented. There is a temptation to try to outguess the assessor and assume that the scene has been set for you to demonstrate a particular technique or set piece. You would be well advised to concentrate on solving the problem as you see it at the time it is presented and to do so in as efficient a way as is possible.

By breaking down the procedure into different elements to arrive at a satisfactory result, you will be able to concentrate your efforts to greater effect.

Every scenario will be different, depending on the nature of the climb and, though it is possible to follow basic procedures, you will invariably have to cope with idiosyncrasies. The real skill of the instructor in these situations is tested to its maximum.

A selection of scenarios follows. These are not exhaustive by any means but should serve to equip you with the necessary skills and procedural elements to manage other possible problems.

Unconscious and injured client

The priority with any unconscious victim is to get down to them as quickly as possible. Ideally this should be accomplished in a few minutes, 3–4 being a reasonable time to aim for. Anything that takes longer than this might be deemed to be inefficient and dangerous. To achieve this ideal requires considerable practice and the ability to work totally unflustered and virtually flawlessly.

Priority must be given to whatever is the quickest method of escaping the system and descending to the injured climber. If your anchor set-up is simple and you are within arm's reach of the anchor, it is often just as quick to go straight into a counter balance abseil as you escape. Having an unconscious victim means that you are most likely to have to descend anyway so, if it is straightforward to rig the counter balance, it is advisable to do so.

Note that the set-up is very similar to that previously described in the simple rescue scenario *Client fails to follow a pitch*, illustrated in photos 14, 15 and 16, which show the set-up for escaping directly into the counter balance descent. By working quickly, given that everything is in your favour, it is possible to complete the procedure within the few minutes' limit.

If, on the other hand, you are a long way away from your anchor, or you have a complex anchor set-up, it is probably more efficient in terms of time to escape the system and abseil down to the victim. Having made your casualty comfortable and satisfied yourself that they can be left, you will then need to return to the stance to set up a retreat which can, once again, be a counter balance abseil.

Never discount the possibility that even an unconscious person might be lowered to a ledge where not only will they be more comfortable but also make your task considerably easier.

It cannot be stressed too highly that speed is of the utmost importance in order to get the casualty into a position where they are able to breathe comfortably and, hopefully, regain consciousness.

For methods of escaping the system refer to vol. one page 144. Instead of backing up the French prusik with a figure eight knot directly back to the anchor, it is preferable to tie it back with an Italian hitch, tied off. This will enable you to convert quickly to a lower and will not present you with problems if the French prusik slips and the rope becomes tight on the safety back up.

The same system can be set up to go to the aid of an injured second who is hurt, but still conscious. Though speed is obviously important, it is not as vital as in the case of an unconscious victim.

Client falls off on a traverse and is unable to regain contact with the rock

This is a good one to be given! It will test your abilities to their max. It is an unenviable situation to find yourself in but, mercifully, a very rare one indeed. Take, for example, the following scenario. A climb has a 5-metre traverse above an overhang. The leader should try to arrange the stance as close to the end of the traverse as possible and slightly above the finish of the traverse. Ideally, the belay should be taken directly above the middle of the traverse if it is a short one, or slightly off centre towards the end, if it is a longer one. This cannot always be achieved.

Photo 17 shows a traverse situation in less than ideal circumstances. Let us suppose that the moment the second unclips the runner above his head, he falls off. Clearly he will fall into unclimbable ground.

A solution to the problem is suggested as follows:

The leader must first secure the rope by tying off the belay device and putting on a French prusik which is fixed to the central belay loop on the harness tie in.

Don't remove the belay device.

Next, the leader should take up some coils of slack from his own end of the rope and attempt to throw a loop to the fallen climber. Having successfully achieved this, the fallen climber will connect the loop to their harness tie on point, preferably with a screwgate krab. As can be seen in the photo 18, one end of this loop is already fixed and the other should be attached to

17 A traverse problem.

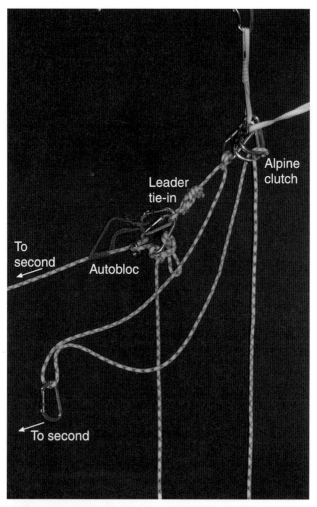

Leader tie-in

Alpine clutch

To second

Autobloc

To second

18 Rescuing a second who has fallen off a traverse.

the anchor with an Italian hitch, or preferably an Alpine clutch (see vol. one page 53).

The procedure now requires considerable dexterity on the part of the leader and great strength on the part of the second. As the second pulls on the fixed rope the leader must take in through the Alpine clutch and pay out through the belay device. (Don't forget to release it first!) By this combination you should be able to swing the second across until he or she is directly below the stance. From here you can hoist them directly up to the belay, using a direct one to one assisted hoist. If your client can regain contact with the rock he or she should climb up and you can take in through the Alpine clutch.

It is an extraordinarily difficult manoeuvre to effect. It is made considerably easier if the second is able to maintain contact with the rock but if they are hanging in space over the lip of an overhang it can be quite problematical. There will be considerable friction and you must not disregard the possibility that the rope may be damaged or, at worst, cut by running along the lip of the overhang.

Once you are both on the stance, secure the second to the anchor, untie them from the end of the rope and pull it through the runners on the traverse before tying them back on to the end and continuing. You will, of course, have to decide whether or not to retrieve the runners. If you do decide to get them back it is easier to ask the client to belay you whilst you reverse the climb, retrieve them and then climb back up to the stance and continue with the ascent.

If, in the very worst case, your second is injured and unable to help, or you can't throw the rope to them, you will need to escape and deliver it yourself or get into a position where you are able to drop a loop.

Be extremely careful doing this. You cannot simply escape the system utilising the anchors above your head. If you do, when you remove the belay device from the live rope to transfer the load to the anchor there will be a straightening out of the tensioned ropes which is accompanied by a sudden shock loading and a certain amount of slack rope.

It is better to re-arrange the anchor so that the loaded point remains in the same position as if you were still belaying the second. To do this you will need to arrange an upward pulling anchor from below and behind you which is connected to the main upper anchors and adjusted so that the load remains in an identical position to that when you were belaying from within the system. Having rigged this complex arrangement, you must then move out along the traverse on the tensioned rope, either hanging from it or by climbing along attached with a cow's tail, to a position where you can drop a loop of spare rope.

If the client is injured you may need to prusik down the rope to them to attach the loop yourself.

Needless to say, this technique requires a good deal of practice!

You have set up a stacked abseil and a client gets clothing caught in the device and is unable to descend – client is unable to touch the rock

Another interesting problem to solve! (Turn to page 67 for stacked abseils.)

The first thing to do is to secure the abseiler so that they cannot move any further down the rope. If you safeguard stacked abseils as suggested later, you will already have the belay device on the rope and can lean back on it to create the necessary tension. Lock off the belay device and put a French prusik on both ropes above the belay device. This should be connected by a short quick draw to your abseil loop.

Put on a second prusik loop above the French prusik to use as a foot loop. You can now prusik up the rope to the stuck abseiler. All the time that you do this the rope will remain under tension, preventing the person from sliding any further down the rope. Photo 8 shows this set-up, though on a single rope.

As you stand up in the foot loop, take in the rope through the belay device and make sure you pull it as tight as possible. As you sit back, the tension should come on to the French prusik which will support your weight while you move the foot loop up to gain more height.

On arrival at the victim make sure that you get as close as possible and maintain your weight on the rope. Try to release whatever has got caught in the abseil device but if it proves a problem do not waste time – cut it with a sharp knife. Just make sure that you cut away from any ropes!

You can now do one of two things. Abseil back down (having first removed the foot prusik but not the French prusik) and, once on the ground, ask the victim to continue abseiling. Or connect yourself to the victim's abseil device with a spare sling or quick draw and then remove your own belay device from the rope. You can then abseil down together with you controlling the descent through the French prusik that remains attached to your harness.

If the client can touch the rock and, maybe, stand on a small ledge or foothold, it may be possible for them to release the offending object themselves and then gradually get their weight back on to the abseil. You must make sure that you keep the rope taut throughout this exercise, otherwise there may be a shock loading on the rope when the client puts their weight back on to the abseil.

You must never ask them to unclip from the abseil device in any circumstances.

You are at the top of a multi-pitch climb and the client cannot finish the route due to an injury

This presents a dilemma. Do you decide to retreat down the crag or spend a bit of time hoisting the client to the top of the crag from where you can easily walk off?

Hoisting presents its own particular problems. Not least, it can be extremely difficult to effect and to operate efficiently. Vol. one contains all you are likely to need with regard to hoisting. Photos 19 and 20 illustrate two other efficient methods of hoisting that might also be considered. Both of these have the advantage that they can be operated from within the system.

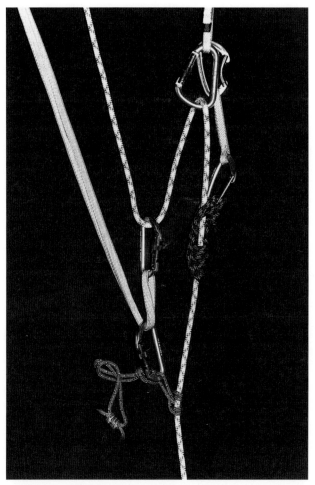

19 5:1 pulley hoist that can be executed from within the
system.

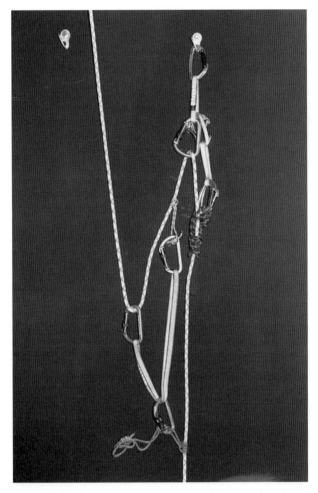

20 7:1 pulley hoist that can be executed from within the system.

5 MIA

Abseiling, stance organisation, multi-pitch climbing and teaching lead climbing

NOTE: *in this chapter the techniques described assume that you will be climbing with two students or clients.*

STACKED ABSEILS

If you need to abseil off a climb with clients the safest and most effective method is to use a technique known as the stacked abseil. This technique requires you to go down first, leaving your client or clients set up on the abseil before you descend. As with all rope techniques it is important to be well organised and methodical in your approach.

On arrival at the top of the climb arrange your anchor in the normal manner. When you bring up each of your clients, get them to clip into the anchor using a long sling. This can be threaded through the harness tie on loops – the same ones through which you would thread the rope. The length of this cow's tail can be varied by tying a knot in the sling at the required length.

Once you have your clients secure in this way, arrange a similar set-up for yourself. Photo 21 shows a sling threaded through the correct parts of the harness and secured with a lark's foot.

Next you must arrange the ropes for the abseil. Be careful to ensure that, as you all untie from the ends, you do not drop any rope. A good safeguard is to attach one end of each rope to the anchor with a knot tied a little more than a metre from the end. This will usually leave you a long enough tail to loop around the abseil anchor and allow you to tie the ends of both ropes together. Obviously, if you think you need more, tie the

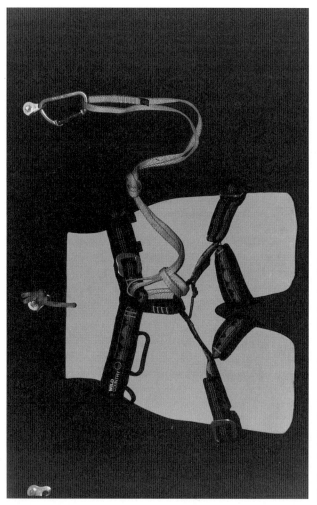

21 Cow's tail attachment for multiple abseil descents.

temporary fixing knot further along the rope. Once the ropes are securely in place you can then untie these temporary knots without fear of dropping the ropes down the crag accidentally.

Decide which order your clients will descend in and attach their belay devices to the abseil rope, one above the other. Normally you will need to attach each via a short extension – a quick draw is ideal for this. Make sure that you use screwgate krabs to attach both to the harness and to the abseil device. Attach clients one at a time, positioning them as comfortably as possible and allowing room for each to stand. As an extra security measure, and for practice in use, you can also arrange for each of them to have a French prusik safety back up attached to their leg loop. Whilst this offers a measure of security and is a good opportunity to practise abseiling with a safety back up you will invariably find that inexperienced students or clients will have great difficulty manipulating the back up and abseiling at the same time. It's a problem well worth consideration.

Place yourself on the abseil rope and make sure that you attach a French prusik safety back up to your harness leg loop. Once you are on the rope you can lean back with all your weight on the abseil rope and be held securely by the French prusik. Photo 22 shows the set up described. Ask each of your clients to undo their sling attachment and wrap the sling around their waist, clipping the krab back into it. By doing this you will have a ready-made cow's tail to clip them into the anchor after each stage of the abseil (photo 23). Unclip your own cow's tail and clear any gear that you are not leaving behind. Brief your clients well on the procedure to adopt for the descent, tell them that it is vitally important that they do not descend until instructed to do so.

Descend yourself to the next stance down (or to the ground if appropriate) from where you will do a second stage abseil. Arrange an anchor for yourself and your clients that is easy for them to clip into. Clip yourself in with the cow's tail. Make

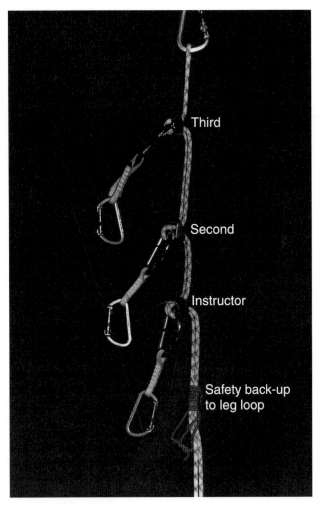

22 A stacked abseil set-up.

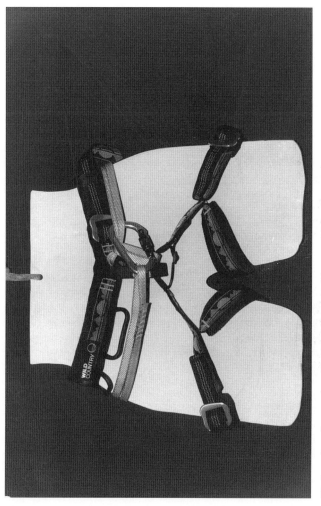

23 Stowing the cow's tail so that it is readily available.

sure that you keep some tension on the abseil rope throughout, as you are basically acting as the anchor person for your clients. By keeping the rope under tension you will prevent them from sliding down the rope.

This is best done by leaving yourself attached to the device you have used to abseil and leaving the French prusik safety back up in place. When you are ready call the first client down. On their arrival at the stance, take their cow's tail and clip it into the anchor. Keep tension on the abseil rope all the time. Once the first client is detached from the abseil you can then call the second one down. The same procedure of attaching to the anchor point applies.

When both clients are off the abseil you can detach yourself and retrieve the ropes. Set up the second stage and repeat the process.

It's worth pointing out here that with this method of stacked abseiling you need not necessarily descend to the next stance in one stage. If, for example, you think that you might go out of sight of your clients, or that you need to keep close by because they are nervous, you can actually descend in a number of stages without the need to rig intermediate stances. If you felt the need to, you could go down to a large ledge at, say, 20 metres and then re-group there before continuing the descent.

Some people leave the clients clipped in at the top of the abseil with a cow's tail which has to be removed before they can descend. This is OK, provided you know that the clients will only undo the cow's tail and not something more important by mistake. It also requires your clients to let go of the abseil rope entirely to sort out gear. It is perhaps better to leave them attached only to the abseil rope via the abseil device and/or with a French prusik safety back up for those that have the experience to handle it.

This method of abseiling with clients is not suitable for anyone who has never abseiled before or who has very little experience of abseiling.

MULTI-PITCH CLIMBING

Poor organisation and planning of stances and construction of belay anchors is one of the most frequently criticised aspects of an individual's skills observed during assessment. On the type of climbs appropriate at this level there is really very little excuse for shoddy belaying, as stances are normally fairly commodious and anchors plentiful.

All that is required is a little careful thought and, more importantly, planning. There are two different scenarios of stance organisation – that required for a guiding scenario, where the instructor will do all the belaying and that in which the clients or students will belay each other. The differences in actual methods of arranging anchors and organising the stance are much less clearly defined, but both require the same approach to safety and simplicity.

The main difference is that in the instructional scenario the emphasis will be on teaching students techniques that they are likely to need in order to go away and take care of themselves. Whilst guiding should always contain an element of instruction, for that will enhance the enjoyment of a day out, the emphasis should be placed on speedy and efficient movement, with as much climbing as can be reasonably achieved in a day.

There is a tendency amongst many instructors to over-instruct. An imbalance between action and words detracts somewhat from the whole ethos of the sport. Whilst we have an obligation to teach, if engaged to do so, we also have an obligation to give clients a good day out on the crags and to give them an opportunity to sample the true pleasures of rock climbing.

It is questionable whether anyone who is shown half a dozen or more differing ways of tying into anchors during a day out will retain the knowledge through to the next day, least of all in the time that elapses before they are able to go out on their own. It is perhaps better to concentrate efforts on one or two methods that can be adapted to suit almost all belays likely to be encountered and to consolidate these skills throughout the day's climbing. Be consistent in the techniques you teach and the student will grasp the principles of safe stance organisation more rapidly. This will make your task easier and allow you to introduce variants as and when appropriate.

Given an ideal stance, you would try to bring anchors together to one central point. Unless the anchor is a sturdy tree or huge block or a fixed anchor, you will always need more than one point to make a solid anchor. The simplest way to bring two anchor points together is to connect the two with a sling.

Photo 2 shows the basic set-up very clearly. (There are other ways illustrated in vol. one, page 122.) By tying an overhand in the sling you effectively create two separate slings. Make sure that you clip into both with a screwgate krab when tying yourself to the anchor.

This system is very simple yet efficient. Problems may occur if the two anchors that you select are too far apart to connect them with a standard long sling. As the angle increases at the point in which you tie into the anchor, the less evenly distributed is the load on each anchor. If the angle between the two anchor points is 90 degrees or less the load will be distributed equally 50% to each. After 90 degrees the loading increases by an undetermined amount and at 120 degrees the load each anchor must bear is the full 100%. Two anchors are normally selected because one alone is not sufficient to hold the force of a fall and it is therefore advantageous to distribute the load so that each has less to hold in the event of a fall. An angle of 120 degrees is obviously undesirable as the anchors must each bear the full force of any any load. This is unsatisfactory if you have chosen multiple anchors because you are not confident that one alone will be able to hold the full force of any load. Many instructors now carry huge slings for just such an eventuality. This is all very well, but they are awkward for clients to carry and, unless you are going to encourage all your students to use one for their own climbing, it may not be a valuable learning experience.

Two normal sized long slings might be a more appropriate method to use. If one is too long it can be shortened to the correct length by tying a knot in it. You might also consider using a snake sling.

The alternative method of tying in to two anchors is to use the rope. Clearly, anchors that are a long way apart will take up quite a bit of rope, but what you will be teaching is a method that is applicable to use outside of an instructional day and one that the students will certainly need to know if they hope to climb on their own in the future.

In terms of stance organisation it is simpler to bring two anchors to one point using a sling. If you decide to use the rope method you will need to think much more carefully about how you position everyone on the stance. It is very easy to get in a terrible tangle!

It is very difficult to set standard procedures applicable to all stances, but there are principles that apply to almost all possible variances.

Always try to position your stance so that you are able to see clients on the whole pitch, including the stance that you leave them on. Sometimes this will mean that you have to ignore stances as recommended in the guidebook description of the route and take intermediate ones. This is particularly important if you think that your clients may experience difficulties in climbing the route. If you can see them, you will be able to encourage them and talk them through a sequence of moves. You will also be able to keep an eye on them to check that they release themselves from the belay correctly. You will also be better placed to prevent problems occurring, such as climbing past a runner without unclipping from it. Furthermore, they themselves will feel encouraged that you are able to keep a close eye on them throughout and they will know that they can ask for help whenever it might be needed.

Position yourself on the stance so that each client can arrive without having to climb over or under ropes attached to the anchor and so that they have as much room as possible to stand or sit comfortably.

Consider the order and direction in which you will move off on to the next pitch. If the climb goes to one side or the other try to arrange things so that they will leave the stance in the correct sequence. This will avoid any possible tangles. When you ask them to clip into the anchor point or points, do so in a sequence that is clear for them to understand. Photo 24 shows a suggested set-up.

If you are going to ask the second to belay the third you will need to make sure that you yourself are in a position to supervise and to act as a safety back up by holding the controlling rope in a way that allows you to lock it off correctly in case they are unable to hold a falling second. This is particularly important if you are instructing novices on their first experiences of multi-pitch climbing.

You will also need to make sure that the ropes are well organised and will run off the pile smoothly and free of tangles as folk climb away from the stance. This is sometimes the most onerous of tasks. It is not so much of a problem if there is a large enough ledge on which to store the ropes, but if you have a small, cramped stance there may not be sufficient room and you might have to lap coil the ropes over a spike or over the rope to the anchor. (See chapter 8 for hanging stances, p. 151.) Here again, make sure that the ropes are arranged in the sequence in which they need to run off – your end off the top of one pile and the rope attached to the middle person off the top of the other.

Stance organisation with two clients requires considerable practice and a methodical approach. Try to do as much of it as possible prior to assessment, as it is an aspect of the MIA that candidates frequently fail to do competently.

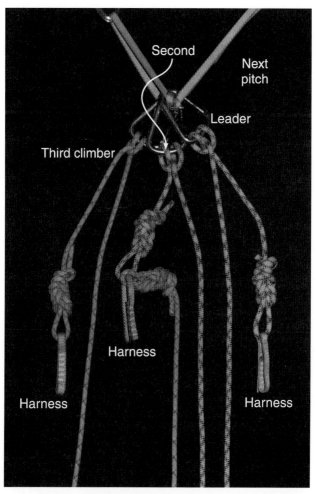

24 Stance organisation. Arrange everyone so that it is
straightforward to move off on the next pitch.

CLIMBING IN PARALLEL OR SERIES

Traditional climbing is conducted in series, that is to say only one person climbs at a time. Guided climbing is sometimes done in parallel, when the guide or instructor trails two ropes, one attached to each client. Both clients will climb at the same time one slightly behind the other. The distinct advantage of this latter method is one of speed.

Any instructional day out should be conducted in series. The reasons for this are simple enough – you are teaching people to climb in a traditional manner and should teach by example rather than use techniques that your clients or students are unlikely to use or even need. The only exception might be when there is a need to move more quickly due to the lateness of the hour or incoming bad weather.

Guiding on the other hand is slightly different in that the emphasis must be placed on climbing as much rock as is humanly possible in a day! To this end you will benefit from the advantage of the extra speed gained by both clients climbing at the same time. But that is the only benefit.

It can be quite unpleasant for the clients if they are in each other's way or their ropes become entangled and there are additional complexities to be dealt with by yourself as the leader.

The least complex climbs to cope with are those that are straight up and down. Ropes will run perfectly and you will be able to protect each client with the rope running directly to them. Unfortunately, not all climbs are so accommodating and anything that involves any kind of diagonal or horizontal traverse will necessitate the placement of strategic runners in order to keep the ropes running as you would like them to. This poses a dilemma. Should you clip each rope into every runner or have separate runners for each (photo 25)? Should you ask one person to belay you on one or both ropes or do you ask each client to belay you on their own rope?

25 Climbing in parallel. Note how the ropes run separately for ease of unclipping from runners.

The answers to these questions vary according to the nature of the climbing. You may decide to clip both ropes into all the runners via the same karabiner. Unfortunately what tends to happen is that ropes frequently get crossed over when the first client arrives at the runner to remove their rope. Better to use a separate quick draw for each rope that you clip into the runner. This means that you have to carry lots of quick draws or reduce the numbers of runners placed on the pitch.

If you decide to place runners alternately on separate ropes you should, for safety sake, ask each client to belay you on their own rope. Placing runners this way may not allow you to position them in the most ideal situation for the client's protection. Remember that runners are placed for three reasons – one is for personal safety in case you fall, the other is for the directional safety of your clients whilst they are climbing, and the third is to show the way.

You will need to decide how best to belay your clients whilst they are climbing. In doing so you have to consider the worst case scenario where you might have both clients hanging on the rope at the same time. Unlikely though this might be, it is nonetheless a possibility.

In order to hold them effectively you must have a good stance with good anchors and arrange the belaying system so that you will not have to bear the full weight of both should they fall at the same time. You can use a belay device attached to your central tie on loop on the harness, just as you would for climbing in series, but you must position yourself so that the load is transferred directly on to the anchors.

You might choose to use a direct belaying method where the belay device is attached directly to the anchor and you attach yourself independently, either to another anchor or to the main one. It is clear that if you elect to use such a method, the anchors have to be a hundred per cent reliable as they will bear the full weight of a fallen climber. However many anchors you use, you will need to bring them to one central point at which you attach the belay device.

The type of belay method you use on a direct belay demands careful consideration. A belay device such as the ATC, BUG or variable controller can only be operated correctly if you stand behind it and are able to lock it off if the need arises. A figure eight descendeur can be operated from below quite effectively, though for maximum braking effect the controlling rope should be kept behind the device.

The New Alp belay plate is designed specifically for this type of belaying. Photo 26 shows the correct way to set up the plate on a direct belay. Unfortunately, as a belay device it does have its drawbacks. It is very difficult to pay out any rope if you want to give slack or if a climber wants to move down to a resting place. If there is any weight on the device it is virtually impossible to pay out rope, or to take in the unloaded rope. This means that if you have one client who has fallen off on to the rope, the other must stop climbing as you cannot take in any more rope through the plate and cannot therefore assure their safety.

On the positive side, the device locks off very effectively and there is never any doubt about holding a fallen climber. It is also possible to leave clients attached to the plate directly to the anchor, eliminating the need for them to tie into it separately. It is advisable to tie off the rope as shown in photo 27, to provide additional security.

When climbing in parallel you are quite likely to experience one other major problem – that of ropes getting twisted. This happens when clients need to step over or go under the other's rope. Whatever the reasons might be for this, and indeed there are few, it happens more regularly than is desirable. To prevent it happening at all will demand that you keep a very close eye on your clients and make sure that if, for whatever reason, they have to cross ropes, they do so without introducing a twist into the system.

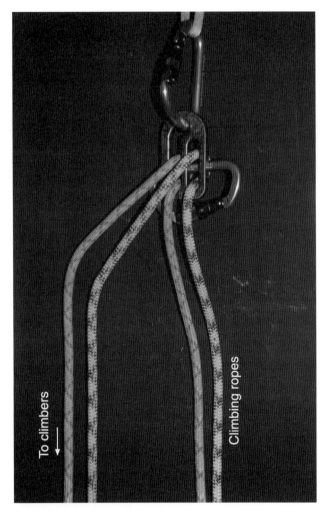

26 New Alp belay plate.

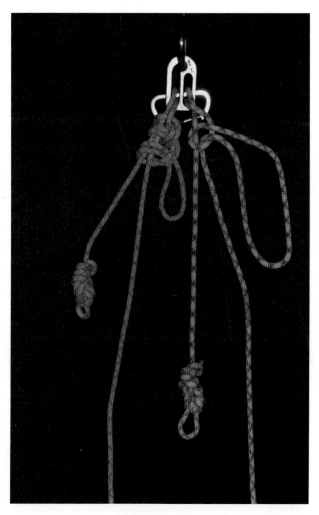

27 Tying off the New Alp belay plate.

Any twists can most easily be sorted out on arrival at the stance and should be taken out as soon as is reasonably possible before more accumulate and create all manner of other problems.

Climbing in series is subject to far fewer idiosyncrasies and is the preferred method of climbing, but it is as well to practise parallel climbing for the occasions when it may be more applicable.

TEACHING LEAD CLIMBING

Anyone who teaches rock climbing will at some time or other need to instruct the skills required to lead rock climbs safely. It is an important element of the MIA and one that you may be asked to demonstrate at assessment.

Before you encourage or permit anyone to practise leading you must first establish that the students are capable and that they have a desire to lead. The decision to allow them to lead must be based on their ability to operate a belay device correctly, particularly as a second safeguarding a leader, and to have a good understanding of the principles of arranging anchors and running belays. Finally you must explain to them that being in the lead on a climb does carry certain risks, particularly of falling, and that there has to be an acceptance of this by the students before you can go ahead. It may even be worth trying to stage a falling leader scenario in a very safe situation or, of course, to use a special weight drop machine where a leader fall can be simulated.

Anyone who leads for the first time, no matter if they have followed climbs of HVS or even harder, must undertake climbs that are technically well within their ability. This is necessary to ensure the highest margin of safety possible. As a rough guide, someone who follows VS 4c competently ought perhaps to begin on a Diff or at most a V Diff climb.

There are different ways to conduct the teaching of lead

climbing. A gradual introduction might take the form of the student clipping into pre-placed runners whilst being top roped. As a progression from this, strategic runners might be pre-placed with the student placing their own in between. Any time a student places running belays, the instructor must be present to assist and advise and to give the final go ahead to use a particular placement or not.

Clearly it is advantageous to try to run a runner placement session from the ground using whatever cracks and features might be available.

When the concept of introducing students to lead climbing was instigated, it was accepted practice for the instructor to solo the climb alongside the student. The instructor would carry a short length of rope with a screwgate krab attached to the end. This rope would either be coiled around the body or carried in a bum bag around the waist. The idea was that it would be a quick and simple method of getting a rope to a student in difficulty – all very well if you can arrange a runner quickly, send the rope down, clip it into the student's harness and attach it to the runner with an Italian hitch, all in the space of a few seconds!

This method, whilst adhered to for many years, is clearly flawed. The instructor is exposed to considerable risk. Even though they might be climbing on ground that is well within the margins of their ability, an accidental stumble or slip cannot be ruled out. If an instructor were to fall they might knock off the student or, at worst, fall and be killed, leaving inexperienced climbers on the crag without the necessary knowledge of how to proceed.

Apart from that most obvious risk, on many climbs there are not enough good holds for instructor and student to share. It might mean in some cases that the instructor is off to one side on VS ground, while the student is on V Diff ground. This, of course, is the worst possible scenario!

Whilst this technique is still used by a very few instructors, by far the most commonly used system of introducing lead climbing is for the instructor to climb the pitch and fix a rope in place at the stance at the end of the pitch, abseil down and then to jumar up the rope by the side of the student who is leading. (See chapter 9, page 164, for techniques of ascending a fixed rope.)

The instructor might place a few strategic running belays on the way up and leave these in for the student. Being attached to a mechanical ascending device allows the instructor complete freedom of movement at all times – to be at the side of the student or slightly above. This level of security is both a confidence booster for the student and also permits the instructor to help out more readily in case of difficulty.

It is a good idea to rig some kind of safety back up for the student that allows the instructor to clip them in if they are finding things difficult or if they decide that they do not feel confident about climbing too far above a runner. This safety back up can be arranged simply enough by attaching a long sling to the ascending device (or a second device) and making sure that there is a screwgate krab in the end which can be clipped into the student's harness quickly and simply when needed. Photo 28 shows a suggested set-up.

Many instructors will take the trouble to back up the ascending device either with a French prusik or a second device. The combination of something like a jumar with a Ropeman above it works particularly well.

The student who is belaying the leader must be well secured and their anchor should almost always include one that is capable of taking an upward pull. (There are exceptions to this rule, of course, and one that springs readily to mind is that of a heavyweight second attached to a great big solid spike above their shoulder level.) If the lead student falls there is then no chance whatsoever that the belayer will be pulled off the stance and you can be assured that they will be able to concentrate all efforts on holding the rope securely.

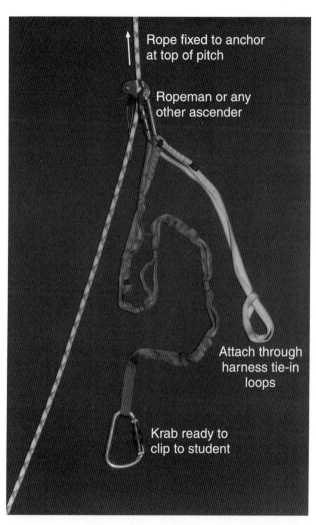

28 Instructor rig for supervising students learning to lead.

As you ascend the rope alongside the lead student you will be able to stop and discuss runner placement and offer tips on how to place them better, or things to consider if extending runners – or any other words of wisdom you are able to impart.

Running belays should be placed at fairly close intervals. Not only will this increase margins of safety but it will also concentrate the practice of placement, giving the student many opportunities to place gear. The first runner off the ground or off a stance should be placed by the instructor and the student's rope clipped into it before moving off on the climb. On stances part way up a climb this will avoid the possibility that a fall factor 2 (see below) might occur if the student where to fall off immediately above the stance and without a runner in place.

On arrival at a stance you can also supervise the selection and setting up of anchors.

As students gain more experience and confidence at leading you can step aside more often and allow them that most valuable of all learning experiences – self-discovery. Knowing that you are on hand to correct mistakes will be a huge confidence boost to the student.

If both of your students have a desire to lead you can allow them to lead through. Before leading the next pitch you will need to go up yourself and fix the rope in place that you are going to ascend on.

It is clear that at this stage of a rock climbing student's progress you are getting much closer to the time when they will be able to take care of themselves. Though it doesn't apply to everyone who takes up rock climbing, this surely has to be the ultimate objective for the instructor – and one of the most gratifying.

Notes on Fall Factor

This is a theoretical measure of the forces involved in a leader fall. I say theoretical because there are many external influences to consider that may reduce the forces likely to be experienced.

The maximum fall factor that can be reached is 2. At this level ropes and equipment might be expected to fail. (There are circumstances where it may be greater but these are not necessarily applicable at this level.) I once had the misfortune to experience a fall factor 2 and can tell you it isn't at all pleasant.

The fall factor is worked out simply by dividing the length of a fall by the amount of rope paid out. For example, a leader who is 3 metres above the second and who falls off before arranging a runner will fall 6 metres. This gives a fall factor of 2. However, this high factor will only be reached if the rock is vertical or overhanging and there is no absorption of the shock loading in the system (rope stretch, climbers bodies and friction over the rock etc.) which is why it is really only a theoretical measure. Nonetheless, all climbers should be aware of the problem, and instructors particularly. Ensuring that there is a solid runner as soon as possible after leaving the stance will avoid the possibility of a direct loading of fall factor 2 onto the belayer.

Interestingly, big falls at the end of a long pitch are quite acceptable! Take the following example. Rope out 40 metres, last runner at 30 metres, length of fall = 20 metres. Fall Factor 0.5! You'd have time to experience the full pleasures of flying during a 20 metre fall.

29 Learning to lead with an instructor in close attendance.

6 Short Roping for MIA

This is probably the aspect of MIA that proves to be the downfall of many of those who fail at assessment. The reasons for this centre on a lack of understanding of the technique and the context in which it is intended to fit within the MIA scheme.

This confusion is possibly because there are a number of techniques that fit broadly into the same category. In 1994, in an attempt to clarify the differing styles and to put a name to each, I proposed the following which have subsequently become widely accepted definitions.

CONFIDENCE ROPING

To safeguard an individual within a hillwalking group who would gain a boost of confidence in an apparently exposed situation by being tied to a short length of rope which is held by the instructor or leader. The instructor may not even tie into the rope. Both will usually move at the same time, therefore not impeding the progress of the group as a whole. The use of the rope is normally unplanned.

SHORT ROPING

The use of the rope to safeguard one or two clients in ascent or descent on terrain that is exposed and where a slip could have serious consequences. The terrain is not continuous rock climbing or scrambling but may have short sections of technical difficulty approaching the V Diff grade (or exceptionally, even Severe). Sections that require safeguarding will generally be very short but could be anything from a few metres to 20 metres or a little more. The instructor or leader will climb the section of difficulty first leaving the clients secure on a ledge.

Normally clients will move over the difficult ground at the same time, tied a few feet apart on the climbing rope. The instructor will safeguard them, using suitable belaying techniques that do not impede efficient and speedy ascent or descent. These techniques are likely to be direct belay methods or, where suitable, a braced stance with waist or shoulder belay. The whole party will move at the same time between sections of difficulty and in less exposed situations.

Occasionally in descent it may be appropriate to lower the clients, either individually or exceptionally both together.

The leader or instructor will not normally place running belays for his or her own protection but may do so for directional stability in safeguarding the clients.

MOVING TOGETHER

The party will travel at the same time over terrain that presents a combination of exposure and continuous technical difficulty or extreme exposure alone. Most commonly this technique is linked with moving along alpine ridges or mixed climbs where speed with a degree of safety is preferable. A competent and compatible rope of two will move together with the rope tight between them at all times. For safety, the first climber on the rope will arrange running belays at suitable intervals. It is hoped that these running belays will go some way towards preventing a tragedy should one or both climbers fall. On arriving at anything of greater difficulty the party will stop and initiate normal climbing procedures.

In a professional scenario where one is caring for a client or clients the position is much more tenuous and requires sound judgement, quick decision processes and sharp reactions that can only be gained through much experience and training at a high level. Consequently this style of safeguarding a client or clients in the mountains is normally the preserve of the guide and not appropriate at MIA.

From the above, it is clear that the domain that fits the MIA is in between that of guide and that of mountain walking leader.

There are two mountain scenarios where the technique is applicable at this level. One is during the approach to or descent from a rock climb and the other is when a day out in the mountains is planned to include a scramble. The techniques and principles are the same for both scenarios. It might be appropriate to begin by outlining the reasons for using short roping and to explain what the principles are.

Scrambling terrain, either in ascent or descent, will undoubtedly feature climbing that requires the use of both hands. It may also take place in exposed situations where there is a very real risk of serious injury or worse in the event of a fall. Usually the climbing is not of a high technical standard, though moss- and lichen-covered rock in the pouring rain will make even simple climbing difficult. As stated before, any sections of actual climbing may be very short and interspersed with other sections of very easy terrain.

Clearly, this type of terrain does not require the use of a more traditional approach of pitching and making stances because it would slow the party down too much. It is preferable therefore to have the rope in place, with everyone tied on to it, so that it can be used as and when required.

The overriding principle is to make sure that the use of the rope provides a good balance of safety but without slowing down progress. To implement this efficiently you must be flexible enough that you can adapt to any type of terrain and use effective belay techniques where appropriate.

Furthermore, you will gain advantages of both efficiency and safety if you remain close to your clients and maintain eye to eye contact throughout. Much can be learnt about the way people react to any given situation and such understanding may forewarn of any impending problem. Such non-verbal communication is worth more in some respects than all the knowledge of ropework acquired.

TYING ON TO THE ROPE

You will not need to use the whole length of the rope but you must ensure that you can vary the length quickly. To do this you will need to coil the rope around your body and tie it off, so that it can be released when necessary. A simple way to tie off the rope is illustrated in photo 81 in vol. one. An alternative method is shown in photos 30, 31 and 32. The method illustrated here is very quickly undone to let out more rope, yet provides an effective locking system so that if you have to take a load directly around the coils it will not tighten up around the shoulders. However, it does have drawbacks, most notably that it will tighten up around your body if you, as the leader, take a fall. This is, of course, the worst case scenario, but if it were to happen, tying off the rope in this way might cause unnecessary injury and jeopardise the safety of your clients.

Some people like to tie off the rope at intervals, so that when you have to drop coils you do so only up to the next tie off point. This is very convenient in some respects but does mean that you have a bulky bunch of knots around your harness tie in point.

Those in your care should be tied into the rope. One person on the end and any others should be tied in with an isolation loop. Avoid, if you can, tying in people directly to the harness abseil loop with a karabiner. This loop is intended to take a static load only and, although it is immensely strong, the manufacturer does not recommend clipping a climbing rope in with a krab directly.

Better to tie an overhand knot in a bight of rope creating a loop about 1.5 metres long to form the isolation loop. Then tie a second overhand knot a little more than .5 metres from the end of the loop. Thread the loop through the harness tie on points and re-thread the overhand to create a secure tie on. The end of the loop can be clipped back into the harness for extra safety (photos 33 and 34). It used to be fashionable to use an

30 Alternative tie off for short roping: Stage 1.

31 Alternative tie off for short roping: Stage 2.

32 Alternative tie off for short roping: Stage 3.

Alpine butterfly to create the isolation loop, but in recent years the overhand has become the favourite. It is an equally strong knot and has the advantage that it can be adjusted more easily to vary the length of the isolation loop and can even be tied or untied without removing the rope from those you are safeguarding.

The distance that you have between the clients will depend largely on the type of ground you are moving over. As a general guideline about 2 metres is just right. Any more, and you will find that slack will easily develop between them, but any less will mean that one is trying to avoid standing on the other's fingers. It is difficult to say exactly how many people you can have on the rope in this way. Much depends on the nature of the terrain. The more people you have, the harder it becomes to manage. One is perfect. Two is ideal, three is manageable, but any more and one must ask the question whether or not margins of safety are compromised.

METHODS OF SAFEGUARDING THE PARTY

At every difficulty encountered you must safeguard the members of your party adequately. The key here is to have a number of differing methods at your disposal so that you are able to adapt efficiently to each situation as it is presented. There are no rules of thumb to apply, other than to be safe. The simplest method of safeguarding someone is to take a braced stance and either to take in the rope through your hands or use a shoulder belay. The success and safety of this method is tenuous to say the least. Much will depend on how strong you are and how heavy your clients might be. A diminutive person may not be able to hold a person weighing 80 kilos with the rope running through their hands.

A secure braced stance (photo 35) is the foundation stone to this technique. You must not stand casually on the edge of a ledge and expect to hold someone who slips. You have to lean

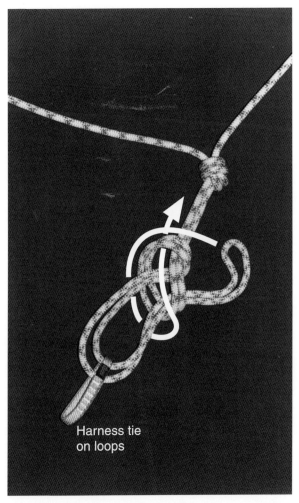

Harness tie
on loops

33 An overhand in the middle of the rope: Stage 1.

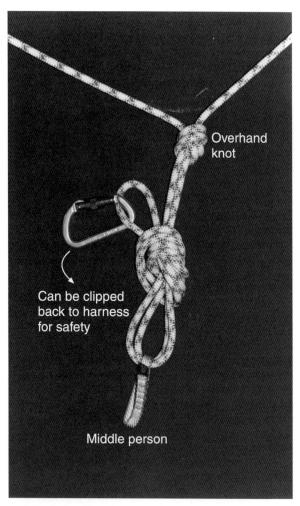

Overhand
knot

Can be clipped
back to harness
for safety

Middle person

34 An overhand in the middle of the rope: Stage 2.

back against the rock or sit down or wedge yourself behind a substantial boulder. 'Every foothold must be a belay' is a popular expression of a colleague of mine. And he's right – think of it like that and you'll not go far wrong.

It is a good idea to use leather gloves that allow you a more positive grip on the rope. If you decide to take in the rope directly through your hands, keep it tight all the time. You should almost pull the client up, but without making them feel that you are giving too much assistance, for they may find it disconcerting.

Keeping the rope tight in this way will enable you to correct a slip quickly before it develops into a fall. This reaction zone is a vital part of any short roping or moving together scenario.

If you feel the need for extra security and holding power you can use a shoulder belay or waist belay. Photos in vol. one, pages 67 and 70 show this clearly. If using the shoulder belay, always remember to have the loaded rope coming underneath the armpit and the dead rope over the opposite one. It is paramount that you do not lean forward because any loading of the rope will pull it off your shoulders. Lean back slightly and dig your feet well in.

It is not advisable to use this braced stance approach on ground that has a high degree of exposure nor where steep scrambling or graded climbing is encountered. Better to employ it where difficulties are short, there is a good ledge below and a spacious one to stand on and the angle is low. For more technical ground and where sections requiring the security of the rope are longer you should use a direct belaying method. These take a little longer to set up than a braced stance and require an element of judgement and imagination.

The simplest form of direct belay is to take the rope in around a flake or spike of rock. It may be obvious, but needs to be said, that the anchor must be a hundred per cent solid. If it isn't and it fails under load the consequences could be

35 A well-braced stance with extra friction generated by
running the rope over a boulder.

catastrophic. Many people fail at assessment for selecting anchors that are clearly not safe. Try to ensure that there are no sharp edges that might cause unnecessary abrasion of the rope. If there are it may be preferable to use a sling instead. Flakes and spikes are the most obvious things to use as direct belays, but sometimes you might find it possible to use other rock features. For example, a large rounded boulder could be used by climbing over to the opposite side from where you anticipate the load will come. The rope running over the rock will generate friction which will help you to hold any load. Small nubbins of rock might also be used provided that they are part of the mountain and not something that is held on with a bit of mud or grass.

Avoid anything that has a pronounced V-shape that the rope might jam up in. Not only might it jam it might also cut the rope if it comes under load.

A sling and Italian hitch can also be used where you feel the need for a more reliably smooth-running direct belay. If you decide to take this option, make sure that you use an HMS karabiner for the Italian hitch. D-shaped krabs hinder the free running of the rope in an Italian hitch and make taking in and paying out troublesome (photo 36).

Bringing the clients up is a straightforward affair. Make sure that you keep a grip on the controlling rope at all times. Any momentary lapse of concentration in this may catch you unprepared to hold a fall. (See photos 40, 41 42 and 43 for the taking in sequence around a direct belay. The same principles apply to taking in through an Italian hitch attached to a sling around the anchor.)

On stances in exposed positions where someone might fall off a ledge, you must secure the party somehow. You must certainly consider your own personal safety for, though you might be quite at ease standing on the edge of a ledge over a big drop, you are still responsible for your clients' safety and that means your own too. Consider clipping in to the anchor

36 Direct belay using an Italian hitch.

using a long cow's tail at the very least in exposed situations (photo 37).

When those you are safeguarding arrive at the stance you will need to have planned your actions in advance. The first person to arrive will be well protected but unless you are prepared for looking after the second or subsequent members, they will be unprotected whilst you secure the first.

There are a number of different courses of action. You can tie off the first person to arrive by securing them around the direct belay. This is done by wrapping the rope several times around the anchor or by tying the dead rope back into their harness. Or you can keep hold of the main rope whilst reaching down to take the rope between the first and second client and then drape it over the direct belay anchor. This is referred to as a counter-balance belay. Provided that the rope sits well down below the top of the anchor and is not likely to get accidentally flicked off, two people can be left on a stance securely in this way.

If you are using an Italian hitch you will find it easier to have a second HMS krab on the sling into which you can clip the rope between the clients (photo 38). To do this efficiently you will need to be very adept at tying knots with one hand (photos 39a and b). Either tie an Italian hitch or clip them directly into the anchor with a clove hitch. Once clipped in the clove hitch can be adjusted so that everyone is tight to the anchor (photos 38 and 39).

Very occasionally you may need to implement the more traditional belaying method of making a stance and using a belay device. If you need to do this it will obviously impede speedy progress and so must only be used in exceptional circumstances where you feel that the party might be exposed to greater risk than is usual on scrambling terrain.

All these procedures take time to implement. The real skill is to minimise the time taken so that efficient movement up the scramble is assured.

37 Direct belay using an Italian hitch. The instructor is secured separately.

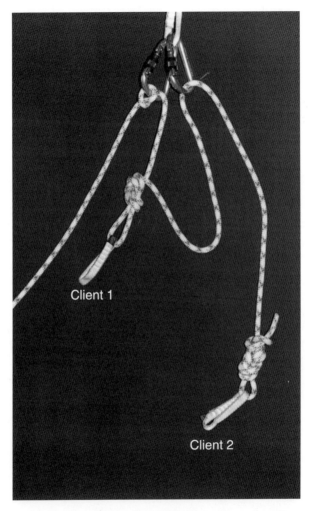

38 Counter balance through krab on the anchor sling.

39a Tying a clove hitch with one hand: Stage 1.

39b Tying a clove hitch with one hand: Stage 2

40 Taking in the rope using a direct belay: Stage 1. Note that
the same sequence applies to the Italian hitch.

41 Taking in the rope using a direct belay: Stage 2.

42 Taking in the rope using a direct belay: Stage 3.

43 Stage 4: go back to Stage 1.

When you arrive at easy sections where people can move without risk or walk to the next bit of difficulty, you can take up the slack rope in coils and carry them in your hand. To do this, coil the rope up in short coils, no more than a foot or so long, beginning at your own tie on point and finishing about a metre or so from the first person down the rope. By coiling this way you are able to drop coils as you need to. (See photos on page 182, vol. one.)

GOING DOWN

Descents using short roping techniques present their own problems. The principles of safeguarding the rope with either a braced stance or a direct belay apply in the same way as for going up.

The main difference is one of route finding. If you know the way down well, this is not so much of a problem, as you can explain to people where they must go. If, however, you are on unfamiliar territory you will undoubtedly need to explore the line to take yourself.

This must be done without the need for you to go first. You cannot safeguard the party well enough from below even if you place running belays. It must be done always from above. To this end experience at seeing and deciding on a route pays dividends. It is unlikely that those in your care will have the necessary experience to choose their own route down.

The difficulties are compounded by the fact that you may need to secure the clients whilst you yourself are descending. To do this you'll need to allow them to make themselves secure. In order to keep a close eye on folk whilst they are doing this you should ensure that they do not get too far below you. Much better to descend in very short stages where you can see what is happening and give instructions as appropriate.

Occasionally it may be preferable to lower people down. If you have a sound anchor, then you might consider lowering both at the same time. Usually you would only do this on relatively low angled terrain where people can support much of their own weight and where you can see them at all times.

If the ground you are lowering down is steep, or involves an overhang, or is at all problematical, lower your clients one at a time.

A way to do this is to untie the middle person from the rope and undo their knot. Make sure before you do this that they are safe, either well back from the edge and unanchored, or clipped to an anchor with a cow's tail. (See photo 21 chapter 5.)

Lower the person on the end of the rope down. If you still have lots of rope available, tie on the second person just below the lowering device and then lower them down to join their partner. You may then be able to climb down or abseil off, using the remainder of the rope which can be retrieved once you are down by untying from the end and pulling it down around the anchor.

If you find that there is insufficient rope to effect this you will have to ask the person you lowered down first to untie from the rope so that you can haul it back up and lower the second.

Very rarely you may decide to abseil. Arrange folk in the usual way for a stacked abseil. You descend first and call each of your clients down when you are ready for them. See chapter 5.

Short roping requires considerable practice before you can do it well. This practice needs to take place in a real situation where you genuinely have to take care of others. It requires those that use it to make a great many decisions based on judgement and familiarity with this type of terrain and the use of appropriate rope techniques.

7 Sport Climbs and Climbing Walls

Some safety considerations

Doesn't it always feel pretty safe climbing on bolts? Clipping in to a sturdy chunk of metal fixed deep into the rock induces a feeling of immortality and encourages bigger air time. It allows you to concentrate on the finer points of style and technique and to push always that little bit further ... The final lunge for the chain lower off or belay is something positive to aim for – a haven at last after the vertical onslaught.

Sport climbing, as it is known the world over, has become one of the most popular aspects of the sport of rock climbing – and justly so. The feel good factor of safety widens the appeal for the less brave, it requires less equipment and, furthermore, one is able to push physical capabilities beyond what might otherwise be achievable on traditional climbs where protection and belays may be sparse or inadequate.

Not wishing to put a dampener on the reverie of such delights, have you ever stopped to think carefully about the things that might possibly go wrong? How problems might be avoided or solved? There are very few things to go awry, it's true, but here are one or two that might give you cause for concern the next time you're contemplating taking a big flight on to a single bolt runner ... Consider clipping a single screwgate krab into the first bolt. If it's not too far off the ground and you need the protection for the first few hard moves you'll probably be thankful for a short connection to stop you from hitting the ground in an early fall. The benefits of doing this however come into play when you are higher up the climb. Clipping in securely to the first bolt will help to ensure that the rope runs correctly through all subsequent runners. It also creates extra friction in the event of a big plummet, enabling the second to maintain a more secure grip on the rope.

Everyone has their own favourite way of racking gear, clipping into bolts and clipping the rope in to the quick draw. It is worth paying a little attention to one or two points. Firstly, consider the direction in which you will be moving once you have clipped the bolt. As a *general* rule it's advisable to have the gates of both krabs facing away from the direction of movement. This will ensure that the load comes correctly on to the back, load-bearing, axis of the krabs. Any possibility that the load may come across the weakest axis or along the gate side of the krab is to be avoided at all costs.

There have been exceptional circumstances, particularly with bent gate krabs, were a fall has resulted in the rope catching in the bend of the gate and actually unclipping itself when the load came on to the rope. The possibility of this occurring is greatly heightened if you clip the rope directly to the krab on the bolt. If you need to clip the rope directly into a bolt, without using a quick draw, you'd be well advised to use a D-shaped screwgate, which is much stronger.

Make sure that the quick draw is not twisted in any way. If it is, it might cause a similar twisting action in the event of a fall.

All these problems can be avoided by very simple prep-aration before leaving the ground. Rack up all the quick draws with krabs facing the same way – it will help too, if you fix the bent gate krab with a strong rubber band. These can be bought or improvised with ordinary elastic bands, castrating rings or sticky tape. It is also possible to buy quick draws with captive eye loops for the attachment of karabiners and these are well worthy of consideration.

There are two methods of karabiner to quick draw attach-ment. Both are illustrated in photo 44 and both are equally acceptable. The only common denominator is to ensure that

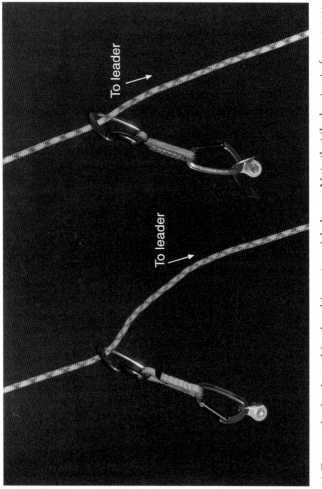

44 Two methods of attaching karabiners to quick draws. Note that the bent gate faces away

the opening end of each krab is always away from the quick draw.

Repeated falls on to bolts may damage the krabs that attach the quick draw to the bolt. Such damage may be seen as burrs or ridges in the krab and, in worst cases, a distinct thinning of the metal may be apparent. This is a particular problem with the more common hanger, as seen in photo 44. Eco bolts and large ring bolts, such as those found on the Continent, present less of a sharp profile. It is advisable to use much sturdier krabs directly on to bolts, as these will last considerably longer if fallen on regularly. If you have any doubts about the safety of your equipment it should be discarded.

Burrs in the bend of krabs can also cause a good deal of damage to quick draws. Repeated falls whilst dogging a climb may cause abrasion of the nylon, with an associated weakening of the quick draw, to the extent that it might snap unexpectedly. Conscientious checking of your rack and changing damaged bits promptly will go a long way to preventing serious accidents.

CLIPPING BOLTS

By arranging your quick draws in some semblance of order you will be able to maximise efficiency and, as a result, will waste less energy clipping the bolt and then the rope into the quick draw. Better to reserve strength for the climb than fumble around trying to disentangle gear from your harness or turn krabs around in bolts or quick draws.

Clipping the rope into a quick draw requires a certain amount of dexterity which is easily achieved with practice. Like so many things, there is more than one way to do this. The following is a suggestion only and I'm sure that as you gain experience, you will adapt or develop your own style.

Photos 45 and 46 illustrate the following suggestion. Bring up the rope draped over your thumb and middle finger to the

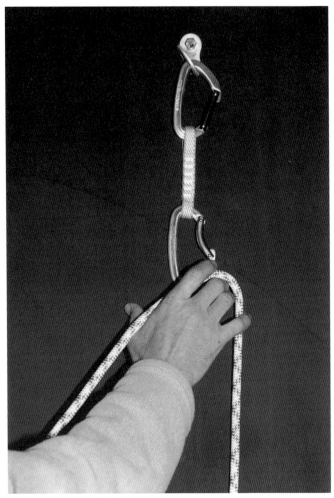

45 Clipping the climbing rope into a quick draw: Stage 1.

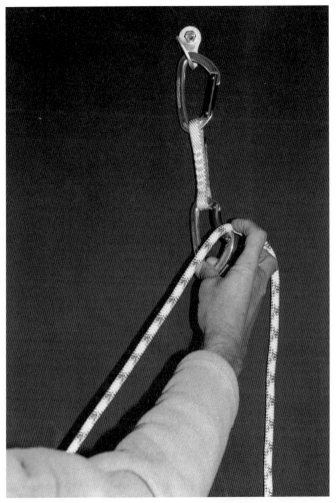

46 Clipping the climbing rope into a quick draw: Stage 2.

krab. Hook your ring finger into the bottom of the krab and pull it under a small amount of tension – this stabilises the krab. Hook the rope into the bent gate and use your forefinger to press the rope into the krab. It takes a milli-second to do this – provided, of course, that your second pays out enough rope!

Remember, too, that bolt hangers can wear out. Particularly ones that are old or made from soft alloy or ones that are subjected to huge numbers of falls – such as those on the crux moves of popular climbs. The unseen part of the bolt can also corrode and weaken over a period of time, though this may not be apparent until it's too late to do anything about it. Be particularly prudent on cliffs near the sea or crags that carry regular seepage. Corrosion occurs mainly on the hidden part of the bolt – that which is buried in the rock.

LOWERING OFF

Lowering off from the top of the climb rarely poses much of a problem but have you ever thought what you'd do if you dropped the rope whilst threading it through the lower off? Once you get a hold of the lower off, clip yourself in to the anchor with a quick draw. You may want to use a cow's tail with a screwgate krab for safety or a couple of quick draws with the karabiner gates turned in opposite directions. If you only use one quick draw with snaplink krabs be careful not to get into a position where you might untwist the krab connecting you to the anchor. Usually, keeping the quick draw under tension will ensure you remain attached.

To avoid any embarrassment fix the rope to your harness with a krab *before* you untie. Pull up a big loop of slack rope and tie a simple overhand or figure eight knot which can then be clipped with a krab into the gear rack. Untie from the end of the rope, thread it through the lower off and tie back into the end. Don't forget to unclip the rope from the temporary tie off on the gear loop before you ask to be lowered down!

Another very good way of going in to the lower off is described below and illustrated in photo 47. Before you use this method you must be certain that there is more than enough rope to reach the ground safely, as some rope is 'lost' using this system.

On arrival at the lower off, clip in to the anchor entirely independently of the climbing rope. A quick draw between the anchor and the harness abseil loop is the best way. Take the climbing rope and thread it through the lower off as illustrated. Tie a figure eight knot in the loop of rope and clip it in to a screwgate krab on the abseil loop of your harness. *Do not in any circumstances clip it solely through the loop of rope formed by tying on to the end of the climbing rope.*

Having checked that all is in order, undo the tie in knot in the rope end. Pull this through the anchor and get your partner to take your weight on the rope. Unclip from the anchor and ask to be lowered down. The photo should illustrate clearly why you must have slightly more than half the rope available.

Many climbers nowadays choose to use 60-metre, or longer, ropes. In Britain there are few crags that require such a long rope but elsewhere there are many climbs that have 30-metre pitches where a long rope is essential.

Remember that if you are very close to the maximum amount of rope available to reach the ground you should ask your belayer to tie in to the other end of the rope or, at the very least, to tie a chunky knot in the end of the rope. This will prevent it sliding through the belay device if the second inadvertently loses a grip on the controlling rope.

Be careful about how you treat lower off anchors. Normally two anchors are provided for the lower off. In the case of Eco bolts these are not connected, as the rope will run freely through them without the need for them to be bought to one central point. Large ring bolts are the same. All other hangers, however, need to be connected, usually with a chunky piece of chain that is connected to the bolts with maillons and the lower

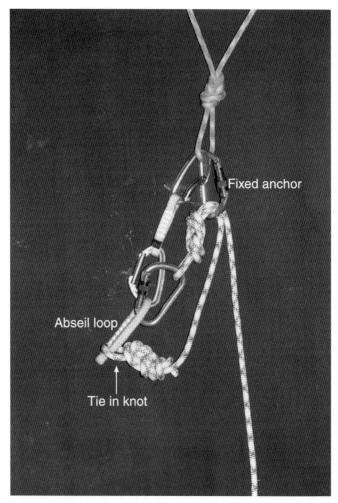

47 Sequence for lowering off from the top of a sports climb.

off point is either a screwgate krab with the gate glued shut or a large maillon.

Make sure that the lower off is rigged in such a way that if one anchor were to fail the other would remain in place. Occasionally you will arrive at a lower off to discover that it is connected with rope or tape and there is a ring through which to thread the rope. The same principles of guarding against failure apply. Make sure that if one anchor fails the whole lot will not fall apart. If you have any doubts about the set-up, replace the rope or tape with new stuff. Rotted or worn nylon has little strength. *Never ever lower with the rope running over or through a nylon rope or tape sling – the heat generated can easily reach a high enough temperature to melt through the sling.*

Photo 48 shows a suggested method for connecting two anchors together for an abseil point. The same set-up can be utilised as a lower off, though of course you must connect the rope via a krab or a maillon if the rope is to run through. For abseiling off you will probably not want to leave a krab behind and in any case there is no need for one.

RETRIEVING RUNNERS

If the climb that you have just ascended is very steep, wanders around a little or is overhanging, it can sometimes be a bit problematical retrieving the quick draws from the bolts. You may need to swing around quite a bit and could even find yourself so far out in space that it is impossible to get enough of a swing in to make contact with the rock.

It is a good idea to connect yourself to the rope that runs through the runners which allows you to be lowered down the line of ascent. This is achieved simply enough by connecting a quick draw to the abseil loop of your harness and the other end to the rope through the runners. Photo 49 shows this clearly.

As your partner lowers you down you will almost certainly need to pull yourself along the rope and in towards the next

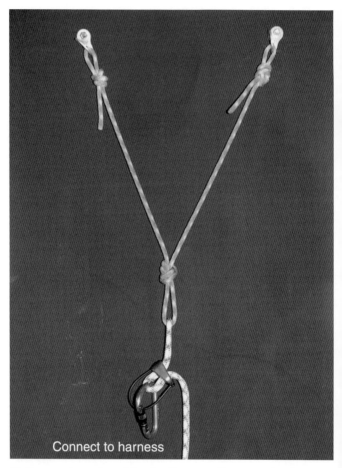

Connect to harness

48 Two anchors rigged for abseil retreat. For re-rigging lower off anchors the same principle applies but clip in a maillon or old krab into the lower loop.

49 De-rigging an overhanging climb. The quick draw attachment helps maintain contact with the rock.

quick draw to be unclipped. If the rock is really overhanging, it may not be that easy to achieve and any strength that you have left after the climb may wane rapidly just getting the gear out!

When you do make contact with the runner try, if you can, to unclip the quick draw directly from the bolt first, rather than take the rope out. It is likely that you will be holding on tightly to the quick draw, relying on it to hold you in position. If you unclip the rope from the quick draw first and let go of it, the chances are that you will swing out of reach entirely.

The technique requires a bit of practice as it is largely a matter of dexterity, massive strength and quick reaction. Pull yourself in as close as you can to the rock and at the moment you are about to swing out again there will be a milli-second when the quick draw is slack – this is the moment to unclip it. Once released from the bolt, you'll then swing out again into space. If it proves impossible to unclip, you may have to get back on to the rock and release some tension from the rope before you can unclip.

On really overhanging routes you can continue in this way until you reach the last one – in effect, the first that you placed on the ascent. Unclipping from this requires a bit of careful thought. The quick draw that you used to connect yourself to the rope through the runners may have to be released. If you unclip the last quick draw from the bolt without doing this the forces on your belayer will be considerable and may pull them off the ground and, as you swing out, the second could be dragged with you.

Take, for example, the following scenario of a climb that overhangs about 3–4 metres over its length. The climb begins on a large ledge, below which is a vertical drop of about 10 metres. The second fails to unclip from the lowering rope that runs through the quick draws on the bolts, unclips from the final bolt and takes the b-i-i-i-g swing. The leader is unable to hold the force of the swing and both swing out into the void.

Neither climber is able to regain contact with the rock and they are both left suspended in space without sufficient rope to lower to the ground because the climb used up just under half the rope length, leaving sufficient to regain the ledge but not enough to allow for the extra height of hanging over the crag below the ledge. This is based on a true story!

The problem was solved easily enough, but consider the implications of the second being unable to retain control of the belay device and there being no safety knot in the end of the rope to prevent it sliding through completely. These are lessons learnt the hard way!

CLIMBING WALL SAFETY

Climbing walls are accessible to all. Their creation is possibly one of the most important developments in climbing history. The number of users increases annually and just about every major conurbation is served by one. Many people who visit walls may only ever climb on walls and may even only try it once. Some will obviously become smitten and progress to climbing outdoors on sport routes and eventually, one would hope, on to traditional climbing.

Because so many users are novices in every respect, including aspects of safety, it is not uncommon to witness a variety of appalling lapses of concentration and rope technique at an indoor climbing venue. It is surprising that so few people are injured seriously. The fact that there are injuries at all is to be lamented, particularly as many indoor accidents can be prevented.

Shoddy belaying technique is perhaps the most commonly witnessed aspect of poor safety technique – particularly when safeguarding someone who is leading a climb.

As with any type of climbing, you are at most risk from injury if you take a fall, either seconding, or particularly leading, close to the ground and most importantly, before you have the first runner clipped. It is a good idea to use an easy way up the first few moves if they are difficult, and clip into the first protection point. You can then descend and try the early hard moves in safety. The belayer should stand close in to the bottom of the wall and as close to the line of the climb without being directly underneath it. If you belay from a distance away from the wall, a falling leader may exert enough force to drag you in towards the foot of the climb. This principle applies equally in 'proper' climbing. In doing so the leader will increase the length of their fall significantly and may hit the ground as a consequence.

The same principle applies as the leader progresses up the climb, though the higher they climb the less chance there is of hitting the ground if a fall occurs. Furthermore, if there are people in the way, milling around at the bottom of the wall or on a climb close by, they might be injured by a falling climber or by a belayer crashing into them.

It is all too easy to be distracted at an indoor venue. Your partner might stop by for a chat, your attention might be captivated by someone doing something hard that you want to do, or you might just aimlessly spend your belaying moments looking around and people watching. Such lapses of concentration on the task in hand might prove to be a catalyst for an accident. It is therefore vitally important to pay close attention at all times.

For this reason you would do well to consider using a belay device designed specifically to make holding a fall much easier. These devices and their methods of application are discussed in Chapter 8.

Consider, too, the weight to weight ratio of the climbing pair. A slight person, weighing in at around 50 kilos, will not have much chance of holding a bulkier person of, say, 80 kilos if they take a big fall. Better to ask someone to hold them down or if available, clip them in to an anchor point in the floor or at the base of the wall.

Anyone who takes along a novice to a climbing wall for the first time should spend a good while teaching the rudiments of belaying before embarking on climbs. Many walls now insist that beginners take a short, usually half-hour, session before being let loose on the wall. This is time well spent. In this session not only must you introduce tying on knots and how to operate a belay device, it is also worthwhile giving novices the opportunity to hold a small fall and to lower a climber using a belay device.

8 Belaying, Double Rope Technique and Hanging Stances

BELAYING – LOOKING AFTER THE LEADER

I'm not very good at taking leader falls – I think it has something to do with being brought up on the old ethos 'a leader never falls' or, much more likely, I'm scared to death of flying. A leader who never falls is an uncommon creature these days. In times gone by, before all the trappings of modern protection equipment, a leader simply couldn't afford to fall. If they did it could result in serious injury or much worse. Nowadays it is a somewhat different matter, provided, of course, your runners are sound, you have the nerve to do it and there's someone reliable holding your ropes.

The leader is totally dependant on a good second who is attentive to needs, manipulating the rope, and who can offer moral support in times of stress. It is not always an easy job and, until you are used to handling ropes and understand the principles of what is required of you, it can be something of a tortuous task.

There are a few basic safety principles to consider. Firstly, make sure that you have a secure stance. Many climbers don't bother to anchor themselves at the start of the climb. In normal circumstances this is perfectly OK, but if you are standing on ground that is less than comfortably flat you should consider some sort of anchor to reduce the possibility that you might accidentally stumble backwards and pull the leader off.

If a leader falls off, the second will be subjected to an upward pulling force. The level of this force will be dependant on many different factors. For example, if the rope is running fairly straight up the cliff and the climb is at least vertical, there could be a considerable force generated. A second who is substantially lighter than the leader may well be lifted upwards and might even be lifted a long way off the ground. On the other hand, the force felt by the second may well be insignificant on a climb that meanders around a bit, on which the leader places lots of runners that introduce friction into the system, and is less than vertical, where the fall would be a sliding one.

By far the worst fall that I have ever taken was on a climb called Flashdance on the slate. The climb is quite serious, in that there are few good runners and you have to do a long rising traverse away from small wires. Nearing the end of the traverse things became a little worrying as the realisation dawned on me that a fall might result in hitting the ground. You just have to dispel such worries and commit yourself. Quite by surprise, both my feet slipped at the same time and I found myself sliding earthwards, fingers burning on the slab. The top runner pulled out of the crack and a crash into the ground seemed inevitable. Quick thinking on the part of my second saved the day. By running down the hill he was able to reduce the length of the fall which was a sliding one and relatively slow (!) and I stopped about a couple of metres from the ground. If he'd been anchored to the cliff I would certainly have hit the ground. I didn't go back up for another try!

This example does not mean that it's advisable always to remain unanchored at the bottom of a climb. Rather it is a lesson which might be put to good use on another occasion.

Paying out the rope can be very trying. It isn't so bad if you are climbing on single rope but double ropes are something altogether different. A good second should always try to anticipate when and how much rope the leader is likely to need and when they will need it. I have often watched seconds who don't even pay out the rope at all, relying on the leader actually to drag it through the belay device. If the leader doesn't complain, it's not a problem, but it's much better to give a small loop of slack all the time – not too much though. If you are a leader yourself you will appreciate more the demands that being on the sharp end place upon the climber and should be more sympathetic to the cause.

Leading a climb can become an all absorbing task. When this happens the leader will rely on the second to pay out the right amount of rope at exactly the moment it is needed. Obviously, it helps to anticipate this need if you can see the leader. A leader who is finding things a bit difficult will often become fairly abusive if the second doesn't pay out enough rope at the crucial moment. This is particularly true on hard moves where protection is needed to bolster failing nerve and waning strength. There's nothing worse than trying to drag up the rope to clip it in to a runner and discovering that you can't get enough of it from the second. The worst case is when you almost have enough rope to reach the clip and no more is forthcoming. After a few choice words you are forced to drop the rope for fear that you can't hang on with one hand any more. This, of course, leaves a huge amount of slack in the system which you hope and pray will be taken back in quickly by the second – a nightmare scenario!

Manipulating a rope through a belay device is relatively straightforward for single rope. Remember that you must at all times keep a grip on the locking rope or dead rope. To make things a little easier when you're using two ropes consider the following advice. Always hold the two dead ropes in a closed grip which is slackened, but not released when you need to pay one of the ropes but not the other. The hand that operates the live ropes can be moved freely around and can let go of one rope to pull the other if required. Photos 50 and 51 illustrate a suggested technique. Photo 51 shows a method of maintaining a grip on one rope whilst paying out the other – something to strive for!

Whether you are climbing on double or single rope you should make sure that the rope is in a neat pile and will run

50 Paying out double rope to a leader, one rope at a time.

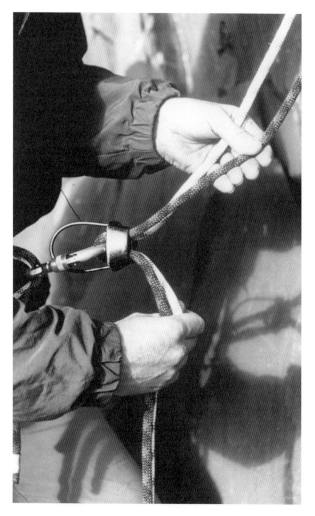

51 When you become more adept, you can hold both whilst paying out one.

smoothly. The all too familiar cry from a second to the leader of 'can you hang on a minute while I sort out this tangle' ought to be an unnecessary one.

The Gri Gri is an excellent device for belaying a leader, though it can of course only be used with single rope. Its only slight disadvantage is that it is heavy to carry. But as it is most commonly used on climbing walls and for sport climbing, this is not really a valid criticism. The device locks automatically when a load is put on the rope. It does this by a very simple cantilever action which grips the rope in a sleeve. There is a handle to release the grip on the rope and this has to be backed up by gripping the dead rope in one hand when lowering. Paying out the rope to the leader is very straightforward and there can be no excuses for not giving enough at the right time! Occasionally the rope will jam if you try to pull it through too quickly. To alleviate this problem make sure that when you want to give rope to the leader you lift the dead or controlling rope above the device (photo 52).

Many people operate the device by gripping the lever which prevents it activating whilst paying out rope, hoping that if the leader falls there will be enough force to activate the locking mechanism (photo 53). In most cases this may work but the certain exception to this is in a slow fall where not much force is felt by the second. The rope can run through the device alarmingly quickly. It should be pointed out that, although this method is used by many climbers, it is not something that the manufacturer recommends.

There are a number of other belay devices available that to a large extent have superseded the original Sticht plate. These devices work much more efficiently in that they are much less prone to jamming accidentally during use.

We will consider, briefly, some of them here.

The Black Diamond ATC (air traffic controller), the DMM BUG and the HB SHERIF, all work in a similar way and are used exactly as you would use the old Sticht plate. (See vol.

52 The Gri Gri – paying out the rope to the leader.

To leader

Grip tightly when paying out

Control / dead rope

53 The Gri Gri – the alternative method of paying out rope to a leader.

one, page 54.) There are idiosyncrasies to each. If you are using 8mm twin ropes, as you might on a big route to save on weight, the ATC does not operate efficiently if you have to hold a leader fall. You really have to grip the ropes tightly even to hold the weight of a climber. The manufacturer recommends that the device should be used on 9mm and 10.5mm ropes, with which it does work extremely well.

The BUG has quite tight holes for the rope in comparison to others. This makes it a very efficient holding device but it can be a problem getting an 11mm static abseil rope through the holes. This is a consideration if you use static ropes to gain access by abseil to climbs on sea cliffs for example, or on Big Wall routes. Once the rope is through the device it does operate perfectly smoothly.

Another interesting device that works along the same principles is the Wild Country Variable Controller. The wedge profile permits two levels of friction braking. If you thread the rope through so that the controlling rope is on the thin end of the wedge you achieve maximum braking effect. This should always be used for belaying a climber, the leader particularly. By having the controlling rope out of the thick side of the wedge the braking power is reduced by a fraction. This is useful for abseiling on double ropes, in particular where friction generated through the device may hinder smooth descent. In all other respects the VC is used exactly as you would any other device of this kind.

Photos 54 and 55 show each of the devices. Photos 56, 57, 58 and 59 show a sequence of taking in the rope when belaying a second. The methods of locking off a belay device illustrated in vol. one are still applicable and Photos 60, 61 and 62 show another method that has become popular in recent years. With this method you do have to be very careful not to let any rope slip through the device as you are tying it off and again when releasing it whilst under load.

Wild Country
VC

Wild Country
SRC

DMM Bug

54 Belay devices.

Another device for belaying is also illustrated in photo 54. This is called the Single Rope Controller (SRC) and is also manufactured by Wild Country. The instructions that accompany the device suggest that a good deal of practice is required before you can be sure that the device can be operated efficiently – and there is a specific warning to experienced climbers who think they know everything! The warning is justified. It does take a bit of time to get used to but, having spent that time, the device is a tool worth using. Paying out the rope quickly to a leader who needs rope desperately is quite awkward to begin with. Taking in is very easy, as is lowering.

The way it works is quite clever. The rope will run freely in and out of the device when you need to take in or pay out but as soon as a load is put on the rope, a cantilever motion, instigated by the tensioning of the rope, forces the karabiner into the slot and jams the rope between a fixed bar and the krab. It is important to remember that the rope does not jam solid and if you let go of the controlling rope whilst under load, it will run through the device. This is an important aspect of use, that must be clearly understood. The device is suitable for use on climbing walls, top and bottom roping for groups, sport climbing and also for traditional climbing when using single ropes.

With all of the belay devices mentioned, and others that aren't, you'll need plenty of time to get used to operating them safely and correctly. If you don't mind clocking up a few hours of flying time on well protected climbs you'll give the second plenty of belaying practice.

55 Belay devices.

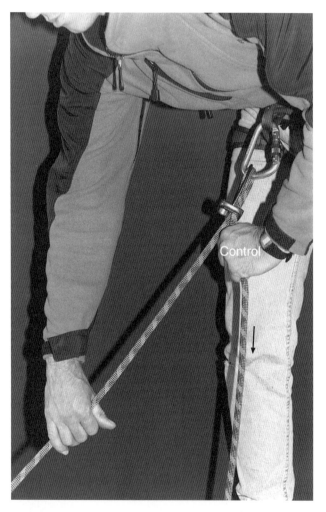

Control

56 Taking in: Stage 1. Reach down with the live hand, pull up and pull through with the control hand at the same time.

57 Taking in: Stage 2. Lock off the controlling rope.

58 Take live hand off the live rope and hold control rope with both hands.

59 Move control hand to below live hand and go back to Stage 1.

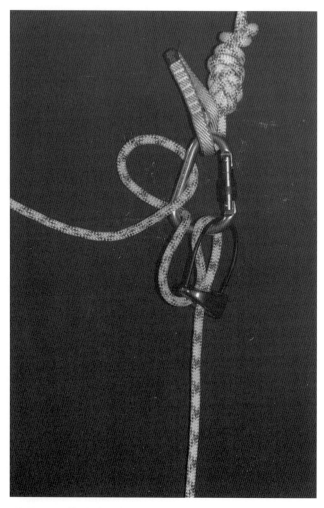

60 Tying off a belay device: Stage 1.

61 Tying off a belay device: Stage 2.

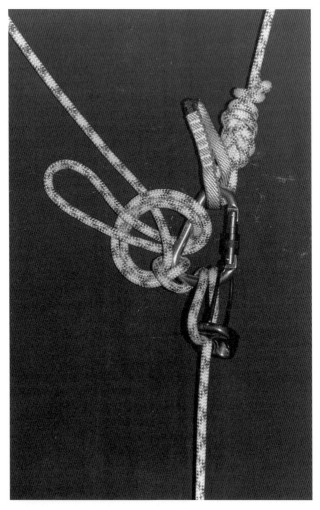

62 Tying off a belay device: Stage 3.

HANGING STANCES

Lower grade climbs are usually blessed with large holds and commodious ledges for stances, big chunky runners aplenty and reassuringly solid anchors. As you progress to higher grades things become much less friendly and very much smaller. There is little solace to be found for a troubled mind and weary body on a tiny cramped stance at the end of a long poorly protected pitch. Neither will you find much relief on a hanging stance high above the ground, secured to your airy perch by numerous small wires, each relying on the other to take their share of the precious load they bear. Nor will you derive much pleasure from the whole experience when your ropes become snarled up in a crack far below you, or they drop into the sea or mysteriously form an unfathomable knot that no text book would ever condone.

But I make it sound far too unattractive! The gnarly experiences are mercifully few but, as any honest climber will testify, they do happen from time to time. Tiny stances and hanging belays need not turn into a nightmare of tangled ropes and awkward change-overs, provided that you arrange them methodically and work neatly.

On any small stance you will generally find it more comfortable to take some of your body weight directly on to the anchor; on a hanging stance you are, of course, forced to place yourself entirely on the anchor. Even the tiniest of ledges on which you can get a foothold will help to relieve some of the discomfort of hanging around for a long time. Modern sport climbing harnesses are not designed for such prolonged periods of hanging about and leg loops and waist belt will cut into places that you never knew could be so sensitive. Make sure that you keep adjusting your position so that cramp doesn't set in for, if it does, on the first few moves of the following pitch you will be moving as fluidly as a wooden marionette.

Where and how to store the ropes on a small cramped stance presents the biggest problem. As a general rule for most situations try not to let it drop down the crag. If you are on the edge of an overhang and the cliff is undercut below you, so that the ropes will simply hang in space, there is little chance that they will get snagged on anything. They may get a bit tangled particularly if there is a strong wind blowing, but at least you are unlikely to get them jammed. The only other time that it's safe to let them drop down the crag is if the rock below you is smooth and clear of flakes or spikes that might lure the rope causing the most hideous kind of jam. In the worst case you may be forced to descend to clear the stuck rope. If your leader is part way up a pitch, maybe on the crux of the climb and you shout up to tell them of the predicament, they will certainly not be very impressed.

Better to avoid the scenario altogether. There are a number of ways to store the rope on small stances or hanging belays. The simplest to use is to lap the rope over your feet – if you can keep them in contact with the rock (photo 63). In most cases this works very well. Keep the laps fairly short, say a maximum of 3–5 metres on either side. If you make them too short there will be so many laps that they could become entangled with themselves, worse than that though they don't support themselves and will keep sliding off. Once one goes the rest usually follow with ever increasing rapidity until you find yourself in the situation you had hoped to avoid! The only inconvenience with this method will be discovered as soon as you want to adjust your foot position to a more comfortable one. Some fancy foot juggling will be needed to prevent the rope from slipping off entirely.

Another way to keep the rope secure is to lap the slack rope over the attachment to the anchor, so that it sits up against your body. Once again, make the laps about 3 metres long, or longer if the way is clear below you. As with the previous system, there is an inconvenience. In this case it makes hand-

63 Hanging stance with the rope lapped around the feet.

ling of the belay device fairly awkward and will need considerable practice to perfect. Photos 64 and 65 show a way to do this. Notice that the rope is stored in between the belay device and the rock – it is much easier to let it run off without snagging.

You can lap the spare rope over spikes or flakes that are close to the stance in a similar way or you can lap it in your hands and then clip it to the anchor with a long sling. Clip one end of the sling into a separate krab on the anchor, pass the sling under the laps and then clip the other end into the krab. This has the great advantage of keeping the rope well out of the way. This method is particularly useful at the start of a climb on a sea cliff where there may not be a ledge onto which you can uncoil the rope.

Whichever system you use to lap the ropes, it is worth making each lap slightly shorter than the previous. This will ensure that the loops of rope do not get snagged on each other and everything will run much more smoothly (photo 66). With all the slack rope piled around you in one of the above methods, change-overs at stances may be troublesome. If you are sharing leads with your partner the rope need not be changed around because their end of the rope *should* run smoothly off the lapping. It probably won't, but that's life! If, on the other hand, you are not swapping leads you will definitely need to run the rope through so that your end is back on the top of the pile. It's good advice not to simply lift off the laps and hand them to your second. Much better to feed it lap by lap to your belayer who can then arrange it neatly.

In order to effect this as efficiently as possible try to ensure that the stance is well organised and prepared for the arrival of the second. This means having something for them to clip into directly on gaining the stance. If you have a number of different anchor points try bringing them altogether to form one central point of attachment. See methods of bringing anchors to one point in Chapter 2, pages 22 and 23, photos 2 and 3, and vol. one, page 122, photo 55.

64 Rope lapped over tie in to anchor on hanging stance.

65 Rope lapping between belay device and ropes to the anchor.

One of the most worrying aspects of a hanging stance, or any cramped stance, is the thought that your second might fall off and the load will come directly on to you. Inevitably, on such stances you are more than likely to be facing into the crag. It is more comfortable to hold a second if you are facing out from the crag but this is rarely achievable when most of your weight is directly on to the anchors. You might be able to run the rope to your second down between your legs. In doing so, if the second falls off, the loading is likely to come directly on to the anchor. But there are many circumstances where this is simply neither convenient nor possible.

A useful trick is to run the live rope through a runner above you. Obviously this must be a hundred per cent solid runner, as it will need to bear pretty much the full force of a falling second (photo 67). If your anchor is absolutely bombproof, and only if, you can run the rope through a separate karabiner attached directly to the whole anchor. In both cases any loading on you as the belayer will come from an upwards direction and the extra friction created by the rope running through the krab will greatly reduce the load you have to hold. It is important to remember here that the krab through which the second's rope will run sits perfectly perpendicular to the rock. If it naturally lies flat against the rock, pulling the rope through it will create a twisting action that will result in a kinked and tangled climbing rope. It basically twists the inner core of the rope inside the sheath and can ruin an otherwise perfectly good rope.

On leaving a hanging stance it is very important that the leader places a running belay as soon as possible. If no decent runner is available, consider using one of the anchors as the first runner. A leader who falls directly on to the belayer can easily generate a fall factor of 2 (see page 89).

It is important to take time out to practise these suggestions before you get yourself into a really scary position. This can be done on any smallish stance on easier climbs, even though you

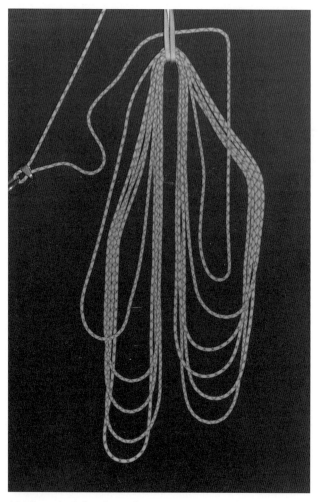

66 The principle of rope lapping using ever decreasing lengths of lap.

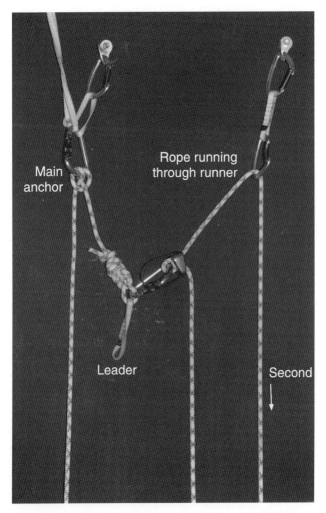

Main anchor

Rope running through runner

Leader

Second

67 Taking in through a runner on a hanging stance. Make sure it's a good one!

might be able to stand comfortably and have enough room to coil the rope on the ledge. Just remember to be neat and methodical!

DOUBLE ROPE TECHNIQUE

In the first volume of *Modern Rope Techniques* I briefly discussed some of the principles of double rope technique. British climbers are probably amongst the few nationalities in the climbing world that use double ropes for the vast majority of their climbing whether on rock or snow and ice.

There are distinct advantages in using two ropes to safeguard a climb. The most vaunted advantage is that it is better in terms of arranging protection. A climb that zig-zags its way up the rock face will be a problem to protect if using a single rope because, inevitably, you will need runners in places that create angles in the way that the rope runs. Not only will this increase the friction and make the rope difficult to drag up the pitch, it will also heighten the possibility that some runners may be pulled out if the leader, or second for that matter, takes a fall.

Using double ropes allows the leader to place protection off to one side of the climb and, by careful management, arrange the ropes to run in relatively straight lines. It also makes it easier to protect traverses for both leader and second with adequate runner placements and reduced rope drag.

There are other advantages. Psychologically it makes things feel a lot safer. You know when you are pulling up the rope to make a critical clip into a runner, that you are not increasing the likelihood of a longer fall if you are unfortunate enough to fall off whilst attempting the clip.

It also makes retreating from a climb or abseiling off considerably more efficient in that you are able to abseil the full length of the rope if need be. Using single ropes only permits an abseil of half the full rope's length.

Tying into anchors is also more straightforward. If you have two anchors, one rope can be tied into each, and even third and fourth anchors are simpler to attach to. This offers added security to the climb.

Belaying is only a little more complex (see page 132) and with a little practice can quickly be mastered.

You do need to be a little more attentive to the way in which the ropes are organised to avoid complicated and annoying twists developing. It is very easy to set off on a climb with the ropes running perfectly but by pitch three have them in such a tangle that the only solution is to untie from one and pull it through the twists. Lots of twists will also have an effect on running belays. If the twists run a couple of metres up the rope in front of you when you are seconding there is a chance that they might pull out runners as the leader takes in. If these runners are critical, on a traverse for example, it may induce a greater feeling of insecurity than might be desired.

Twists are introduced into the system every time you turn a complete circle. Tie in to two ropes and see what happens when you spin around three or four times. Imagine doing this whilst on a climb or particularly on a stance and you will soon realise how those twists develop so 'mysteriously'. Being aware of the problem goes a long way to preventing it happening in the first instance.

Try to make sure that you run the ropes through at the end of each pitch. Do them individually if you can be bothered or at least together and separate them by running one finger in between each rope as you do so. If twists are apparent one of you can spin around to unravel them. Don't do it too fast or you'll get dizzy and fall off the ledge!

Take a good look at the pitch before you set off and plan where you hope to place runners and which rope you will use where. A moment's planning pays dividends in the long run.

Double ropes provide considerably safer opportunities to protect both leader and second on traverses. Using a single rope may require you to miss out using a crucial runner because to place it would create too much friction or pull out other more critical runners. Such problems can be avoided by extending runners with long slings to decrease the angles through which the rope runs, but doing so sometimes means that a fall may be longer than you would like. Double ropes permit better use of runners in such situations and, though sometimes runners may need to be extended, the occasions are far fewer.

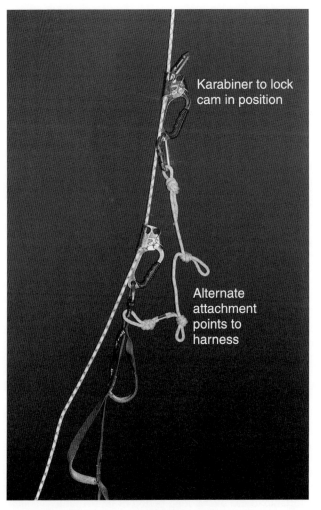

Karabiner to lock
cam in position

Alternate
attachment
points to
harness

68 Traditional method of ascending a fixed rope. Note that the
foot ascendeur is connected back to the harness.

9 Ascending a Fixed Rope

In vol. one the techniques of ascending a fixed rope were discussed briefly. Though all that was said remains valid, there are one or two further suggestions worth making.

Whenever you have a need to ascend a fixed rope other than in an improvised rescue scenario, you should consider using some kind of a mechanical ascending device. Such devices not only offer increased security but they are also much more efficient to use.

Occasions that demand the use of mechanical devices include those in which an instructor is teaching a student to lead and those where you are on a multi-day climb that requires you to descend and re-ascend on several occasions. Both these require a slightly different approach to the method in which you attach yourself to the devices.

For ascending a fixed rope when climbing on big walls, it is advisable to connect yourself via the sit harness to both devices as a sensible safety measure. Photo 68 shows a suggested method of doing this. You would be well advised to use a chest harness connected to the sit harness and to link the two together to form on central point of attachment. This will make long ascents considerably more comfortable and provides a better positioned point of attachment if you have a heavy load on your back.

The length of the safety back up attachment to the foot ascendeur is fairly critical and should be adjusted so as not to impede the distance that you can move the foot ascendeur up the rope for maximum efficiency.

There are a large number of devices available for ascending a fixed rope. Those that incorporate a handle are the most comfortable to use over a long period of time. Lighter versions are also available that do not feature a handle and are worth considering for short sections of ascent. Petzl is perhaps the most well known brand name and offers a range of devices which will suit any situation you are likely to encounter.

The Croll is an interesting device that is designed to connect between a sit harness and a chest harness. Photo 69 shows how the Croll should be used. It is a very efficient device in that there is no need to move it up the rope by hand. As you stand up in the foot loop the device slides along the rope. It is important to fix the Croll securely at both ends, the top to a chest harness and the bottom to the sit harness. Ensure that there is very little slack in the connection. This will help it to operate as efficiently as it is designed to do. Another important development is the Ropeman from Wild Country. This remarakable little device is incredibly simple to use and offers a degree of safety and efficiency unsurpassed for its diminutive appearance. It weighs only a few grammes and can be carried easily in place of a prusik loop, over which it has considerable advantage, particularly in aspects of safety. Photo 70 shows the Ropeman attached to the rope. As a device to use in emergency prusiking, such as crevasse or crag rescues, it is particularly useful.

If the rock is low-angled where you can support a good deal of your body weight on your feet, you need only attach yourself to the Ropeman via the abseil loop on your harness. Make the attachment fairly short. As you step up the rock face, take hold of the fixed rope below the device and pull it upwards. The rope will run smoothly through the Ropeman and you can feel secure, knowing that you are able to lean back on it at any time and it will lock on the rope.

If you have two devices and the ground is much steeper, attach to the top Ropeman via your harness and use the bottom one for a foot loop. Don't make the connection to the sit harness too long, about level with your chest is plenty. The foot loop attachment should be as short as you can comfortably stand up in. Move the top Ropeman up by sliding your hand under the cam and pushing it back so that it releases.

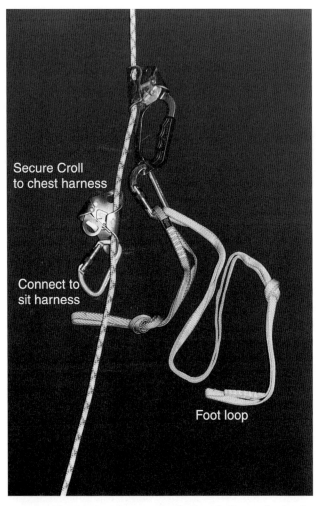

Secure Croll
to chest harness

Connect to
sit harness

Foot loop

69 Ascending a rope using a Croll. The Croll must be firmly attached to a chest harness of some sort.

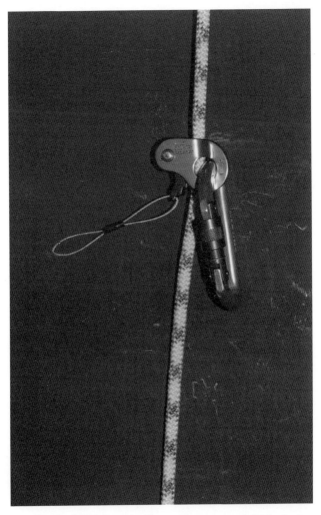

70 The Wild Country Ropeman – a superb little device.

To move the foot one up, keep a little tension on the device and take hold of the rope below the device. By pulling upwards on the rope the Ropeman will slide up perfectly.

There is no reason why the Ropeman could not be used by instructors teaching lead climbing (see page 84), instead of a more traditional type of ascendeur. The grip on the rope is just as efficient and the strength of the device as adequate. If you are not happy to do this, it can be used as a back up to another ascending device by placing it above the main ascendeur and connecting the two together with a karabiner.

71 Ascending a fixed rope. When carrying a big pack always wear a chest harness.

10 Retreating from Climbs

Just as there will be success on climbs, there will also be failures. Learning to cope with failing on a climb is a difficult thing, particularly if the route is one you've aspired to, dreamt about doing and sought as much information on as you can.

Talking about failure seems a very negative thing but when you're out on your own having to make decisions about backing off a route, it takes on monumental importance.

One of my early failures on a climb was on a route at the Roaches when I was at college in Buxton. I was the only climber on our course and keen to encourage others to climb so that I would always have partners to go out with. I can't remember for the life of me the name of the climb but it was away left of the Sloth area. It was a bleak and miserable autumn day with a fine drizzle dampening everything but our enthusiasm. Not having a guidebook, we scoured the crag for likely looking easy lines and found one that looked possible. It began reasonably enough but the rock was slimy and cold. About 10 metres or so off the ground, maybe less, further progress became a matter for bravery that I was unable to muster and I decided to retreat.

I had put a sling around an almost horizontal spike of rock for protection and worked out that, if I took that off, I could put the rope around it and be lowered off by the guys holding the rope below. They didn't know how to use a waist belay so all three of them just held on to the rope. All went well until about 3 metres off the ground when one of them noticed the rope gradually creeping off the spike. We stopped and pondered our next move and decided that it would probably be OK until I reached the ground. Of course, it wasn't – just as soon as they resumed lowering me it popped right off. I fell down on top of my companions and all four of us tumbled and rolled down the muddy slope in a tangled heap with much mirth and merriment. Only one of them ever went climbing again after that. Another instructional success!

Retreating off a pitch when you're part way up and have reached the point where you can get no further can be quite harrowing. If you have a good runner you may well decide to lower off that and then let your partner make an attempt. If he or she doesn't fancy having a go at leading the pitch you'll either have to down climb taking out all the runners as you descend or, if the prospect of down climbing is too daunting, you'll need to lower off a piece of gear, or even two connected together.

This may present you with a bit of a dilemma on two counts. One is of pride. Anything you leave behind is a reminder of your failure and a symbol of a failure for others to gloat upon. The other is the loss of an expensive piece of equipment that might have been hard to come by. Put both out of your mind, for the thing that matters most of all is that you get off safely and return to climb another day.

When being lowered off you should always be lowered with the rope running through a karabiner. Never be tempted to run the rope through a nylon sling or through the wire of a nut. Nylon has a very low melting point and with the added weight and the friction of the rope running over a nylon sling it is possible to generate sufficient heat to melt through the sling. Lowering through a wire doesn't create the same problems but the rope will not run smoothly over such a tiny radius and you may well damage the climbing rope – a much more expensive item of gear to replace.

It is far better to leave behind a krab. It need not be one of your best though – in fact make sure it isn't. It's quite a good idea to carry your nut key on an old krab which you could use for just such a purpose. Although you might lose a nut or a sling at least you'll feel that that's all you've lost.

If you are part way up a multi-pitch climb, say on the third pitch, once you've been lowered back to the stance you'll then need to find an escape route that is considerably easier or, if none exist, retreat to the ground by abseil.

It is quite likely you'll need to leave gear behind on each abseil. If you can get back to the ground in one long abseil, then all is well and good and you'll lose only minimal gear. If, on the other hand, you're too high off the ground to do this, you'll need to go down in stages. Unless you have a clear view of where to go and can see likely places to use as staging posts, it may be safer to retreat down the line of ascent. This becomes less preferable if the route you climbed weaves its way all over the crag.

When you retreat by abseil in this way there is no need to leave a krab behind on each anchor. The rope will be doubled through the anchor and will only run over the nylon sling when you retrieve it. At this point you no longer need the sling and so any heat generated that might melt the sling is of little consequence. Of course, you may not have to leave anything behind if there are suitable rock spikes to abseil off, or maybe trees. If you use spikes in this way make sure that the first person down tests the rope to see that it will pull around the spike before the last person sets off. If it doesn't, you may well have to leave a bit of gear in place to make the retrieval of the rope less troublesome.

On long multi-pitch descents off big routes, and particularly the most popular ones, you may find that all the equipment is in place. There is a climb on the Grauewand for example, just above the Furka Pass in Switzerland, where the abseil descent has been rigged with two large ring bolts connected with a plate that has an eye in the end for clipping in to. This is the most luxurious of pre-set rap stations. Many others may feature in-situ gear connected with a chain or with slings. Regardless of the set-up each should be checked before you use them, rather than blindly trusting to them.

In the case of all metal anchors there is very little that can go wrong, unless of course they are old and rusted through.

Slings, however are a very different matter. Nylon deteriorates over a period of time when exposed to the UV rays of the sun. Any piece of in-situ gear that is faded ought to be treated with suspicion. To check the degree of fading unravel a bit of the knot and see what the original colour of the sling was. Similarly, if the rope is to be threaded through the sling directly, some heat will be generated when ropes are pulled through during retrieval. This heat may cause some melting of the nylon and this could weaken the sling considerably.

If you need to replace the sling do so with careful consideration not just to how you will use it but also how others might use it in the future. Normally at least two anchors will be used. When connecting the two make sure that you arrange the sling so that, if one were to fail, your abseil rope will not detach itself from the other. Photo 48 shows a suggested set-up. There are other ways to connect the two to one point and the principles remain the same for whatever method you choose.

I once, to the horror of my partner, suggested that we abseil off a lace from my rock boot. It was 4mm nylon boot lace and we did thread it through the peg about eight times before joining the ends together. Nonetheless, when I think back on it now it was a pretty stupid thing to have done, even abseiling off one old peg was daft enough. It came down to the fact that I didn't want to leave anything of value behind.

From then on, to cope with such eventualities in the future, I began carrying a couple of short prusik loops made up of 6mm accessory cord – and have been doing ever since. Boot laces aren't what they used to be anyway . . .

Retreating off bolted climbs when you fail can be a bit troublesome. Bolt hangers that allow you to clip in two karabiners at the same time, or even to thread a rope through, are much more convenient to retreat from without leaving gear behind. Take the most simplistic scenario: a bolt climb with large ring bolts or DMM Eco anchors. With these it is a simple enough matter to clip yourself to the bolt with a short cow's tail attachment made up from a quick draw. Secure the climbing rope to your harness and then untie from the end of the rope. Thread the end through the bolt and tie back on. Ask your partner belaying you to take all your weight on the climbing rope and then unclip the cow's tail from the bolt. Some jiggling of krab and rope may be needed but this is easily accomplished. You can then be lowered through the bolt and collect the other quick draws on the way down.

If you are climbing a sport route that has any other type of hanger you have bigger problems and will need to leave something behind to lower off, though if the crag is easily accessed from above, you can simply nip around to the top and abseil down to retrieve the lost runner. Or you might be able to ask the next person to climb the route if they would kindly get it back for you.

If neither of the above solutions is possible you should leave a krab behind on the bolt and be lowered off that. You may be loathe to leave a good krab behind, in which case you must take one that you are prepared to leave, unclip the quick draw and then clip the disposable krab into the bolt hanger, with the climbing rope already clipped in. To do this you'll need to have enough strength to hold yourself on the rock whilst re-arranging the gear.

Another way to retreat is to clip yourself into the bolt with a cow's tail. Take a short length of cord/prusik loop and thread it through the hanger. Take the climbing rope and tie the two ends of the cord together, thus securing the rope. It is probably advisable to thread the cord through twice so that you have double the strength.

Next, pull the rope through, so that you have enough to reach the ground or the stance below on the doubled rope. Having done that you can attach yourself to both ropes in preparation to abseil off. You will, of course, need a device to descend on, normally your belay device. Once the abseil is rigged you can untie from the end of the rope and let it drop to the ground. Unclip from the bolt and cow's tail attachment, clear any other gear and descend. Photos 72, 73 and 74 show the procedure.

This same principle can be applied to a retreat off any kind of runner, provided, of course, that you are happy with the placement!

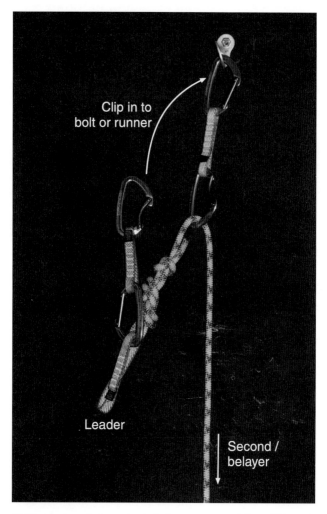

72 Retreating from a single bolt or runner whilst still hanging on it: Stage 1.

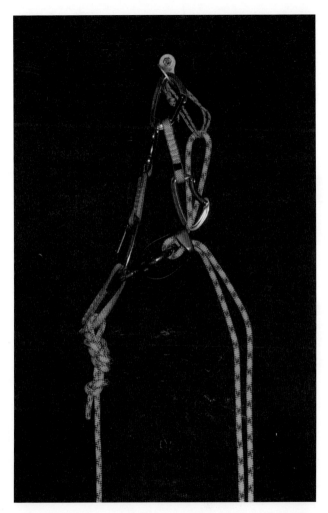

73 Retreating from a single bolt or runner whilst still hanging on it: Stage 2.

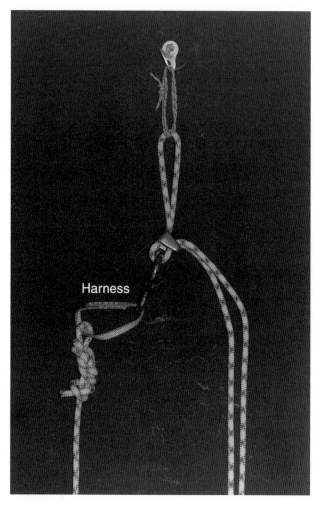

74 Retreating from a single bolt or runner whilst still hanging on it: Stage 3.

11 Miscellany

TENSIONING ROPES FOR A TYROLEAN OR SAFETY LINE

In the first volume, *Modern Rope Techniques*, I suggested that ropes could be tensioned using pulleys at each turning point in the tensioning system. Whilst this makes it considerably easier to attain the required tension, the pulleys used have a limitation to their breaking strength. This limitation is imposed by the strength of the axle on which the pulley rotates.

If you do not have pulleys or those that you have do not fall within acceptable safety margins, the technique illustrated in photos 75, 76 and 77 is a perfectly good method of tensioning ropes.

The Alpine butterfly knot is tied as far down the rope as you can possibly reach. Try to make the loop formed by the knot fairly small, just large enough to squeeze your fist through.

Attach a screwgate karabiner. Take the rope from the knot and pass it through a screwgate on the anchor, then take it back to the Alpine butterfly krab and clip it in. You now have a pulling system. It might require a number of people to pull on the rope to achieve the required tension.

Once the rope is as tight as you need it to be, 'marry' the ropes and then secure them by threading a bight of rope through the krab at the anchor and tie a number of half hitches around the three tensioned ropes. You can include the fourth if you wish but there is really no need.

As stated in vol. one, it is important to try to use low-stretch ropes for this type of work as they are considerably more robust and capable of the loads exerted on them.

Over a period of use, some tension may be lost and you'll need to re-tension the rope from time to time. This is effected

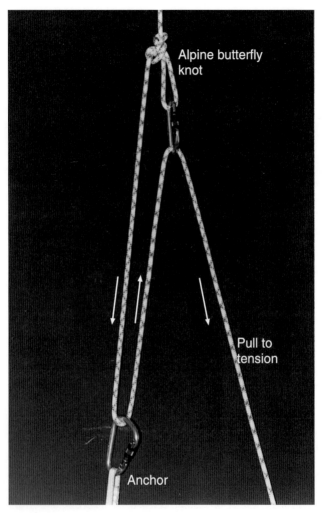

75 Tensioning ropes: Stage 1.

76 Tensioning ropes: Stage 2.

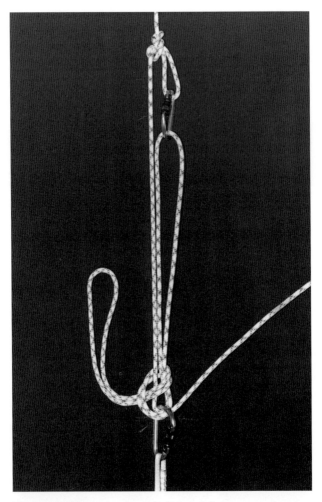

77 Tensioning ropes: Stage 3: 'Marry' the ropes and secure with half hitches.

easily by releasing the half hitches whilst 'marrying' the ropes together and then getting help to pull more tension into the system. The Alpine butterfly will be extremely tight after use and may be difficult to undo. If the ropeway has been used to cross a river or a gorge and you need to get the rope across to one side without getting it wet or without the risk of getting it stuck around a rock or a tree, for example, the best way to do it is as follows.

Decide which side the rope needs to end up on. On that side take in all the rope until the person left on the other side has only the end of rope to hold. Both sides then pull the rope until there is tension in it, but only holding it in their hands. On a pre-arranged signal the person on the opposite side lets go of the rope and, in theory, it should go whistling over to the side you want it to finish up on. Obviously, those receiving the rope must be prepared for the sudden slackness otherwise they will fall flat on their backsides – usually accompanied by much mirth and merriment from onlookers.

SAFETY LINES FOR TRAVERSES

In any situation, such as a sea level traverse for example, where you need to rig a horizontal safety line, those for whom the line is rigged will need to have some method of clipping in. There are various ways of doing this and the simplest is to clip in with a sling attached to the harness.

It is vitally important that you consider carefully how the line is rigged. For safety it is preferable not to have too much slack in the system, otherwise the purpose of the line is defeated. Clearly, the line is there to hold someone if they slip off. To do this the line needs to have a reasonable amount of tension in it, otherwise the fall could be considerably longer than is desired and might lead to injury.

It is no good, therefore, to stretch a rope between two points that are a long way apart, 20 metres for example. In fact, I would venture to suggest that the maximum distance acceptable ought to be around the 6-metre mark, particularly if you are using climbing ropes to rig the safety line. Anyone loading on a horizontally placed line will inevitably introduce considerable stretch and this must be considered when rigging. Low stretch ropes present less of a problem in this respect but nonetheless the same considerations must be applied. You must therefore, make sure that the rope is anchored securely and at frequent intervals.

Anchors placed along the traverse would, ideally, be above the line of travel. This is not always possible. Any anchors placed on the line of travel should be placed so that they cannot be lifted out accidentally. To this end you might need to rig an upward pulling anchor to hold the downward pulling one under tension, so that it remains solidly placed.

The knot that you use to attach the rope to each of these anchors could either be an overhand, a figure eight or an Alpine butterfly. It matters little, though the overhand, and particularly the Alpine butterfly, are more suited to taking a load in either direction.

The change-over at each anchor point is effected with greater safety if you arrange a cow's tail similar to that shown in photo 78. By using this set-up you will be secure on one rope whilst you clip into the next. As you arrive at an anchor the spare cow's tail is clipped in and the screwgate secured before you unclip from the other.

Not all safety lines rigged this way are horizontal. Inevitably there will be sections of vertical ascent or descent. The Via Ferrata of the Italian Alps are classic examples of this.

If you take a fall in ascent or descent you will obviously fall as far as the anchor point below you. In some cases this might be a considerable distance. The forces generated by such a fall are enormous. For example, if the length of sling attachment is a metre long and you fall 5 metres the fall factor (see page 89) is 5. It is made doubly worse by the fact that there is no shock

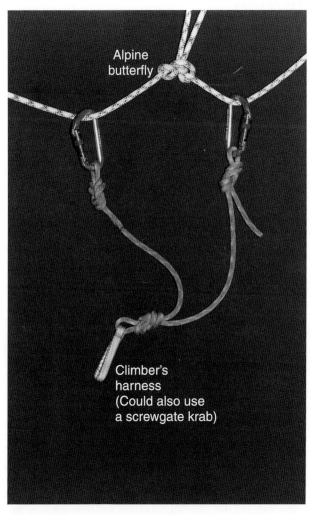

Alpine
butterfly

Climber's
harness
(Could also use
a screwgate krab)

78 A simple cow's tail attachment for safety line traverses.

absorption in the system. If the sling that attaches you to the line doesn't break, your body is almost certain to.

There are a number of devices that are specifically designed to absorb the shock of such a fall. The least complex of all is the ZYPER from Petzl. This is a very simple set up constructed of a length of rope with pre-formed loops in either end. Shock absorption is effected by a simple twist through the link that is attached to the harness. Basically, as the load comes on to the lanyard, the rope slips gradually through the link, absorbing a great deal of the shock load.

Such devices cannot be improvised easily from normal climbing equipment.

RETRIEVABLE SINGLE ROPE ABSEIL

Quite when this technique may be useful is difficult to say with any certainty. It's one of those things that may come in useful sometime – like that bizarre tool stashed away in the shed that'll come in handy if I never use it!

However, I did hear an interesting story from a mate of mine who was climbing in Spain once. Arriving at the top of a multi-pitch climb, he waited to one side while the pair in front rigged their abseil descent. The first climber went down and the second climber attached himself to the rope to begin the descent. As he leant backwards on to the rope my mate noticed that he was only attached to one rope and frantically lunged forward to save him, screaming, 'Stop, stop, you're only on one rope!' The climber turned to him, slightly bemused by the show of concern, and said, 'I know. My belay device will only take one rope.' He'd rigged the rope out of sight of my mate who wasn't able to see the whole set up. Photo 79 shows the method clearly.

There are two vitally important considerations. The first is that the ring or maillon or krab that the rope is threaded through must not have too large a hole, otherwise the knot

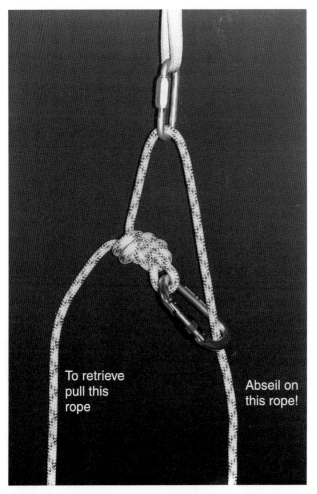

To retrieve
pull this
rope

Abseil on
this rope!

79 Retrievable single rope abseil. Make sure that you abseil on
the correct rope!

might slip through as you descend. Whilst it will never become entirely detached, it may become jammed in the hole or cause confusion over which rope to pull.

Most important of all, though, is to ensure that you abseil on the correct rope – the opposite side to that in which the knot is tied. The consequences of going down on the wrong rope do not bear thinking about.

Index

Figures in *italic* indicate illustrations.